MW01089962

What Did Jesus Say?

Why the Bible Does Not Condemn Homosexuality

What Did Jesus Say?

Why the Bible Does Not Condemn Homosexuality

By K. Darnell Giles

A Project GBC Publication

Published by:
A Project GBC Publication

ISBN: 1-440-47898-8
EAN-13: 978-1-440-47898-7

Unless otherwise indicated, Scripture is taken from The Holy Bible,
New King James version, © 1982

Many of the names of the people in this book have been changes to
protect their privacy.

Cover Design: Tony Maietta of Mark Street Design
www.markstreetdesign.com

Dedication

Jesus, You are the one and only. You have proven it and I am forever grateful.

Much love, respect and appreciation to my family and friends, who through my personal challenges, have continued to love me and show me how to love others, without judgment, from a true heart.

JP – We will miss your gregarious laughter and big bright smile. You were a Godsend to our family.

D – You know words are inadequate to express my love for you. We are forever knit by our blood and His blood.

About the Author

K. Darnell Giles has spent much of his adult life grappling with the seemingly contradictory issues of his life – his identity as a born-again Christian and his same sex orientation. As a licensed minister within a conservative church, he felt that he lived a life of hypocrisy, attempting to "be straight", while trying to suppress his same-sex attractions that were not dissipating.

What Did Jesus Say? is his second self-published work. For many years, K. Darnell believed what many in the Christian community believe, that his homosexual orientation was unnatural and sinful. His previous book, *Gay, But Not Happy*, discussed ways to overcome homosexuality and become an "ex-gay" Christian, a position he no longer holds. One of the dichotomies of his life has centered on his image as an 'ex-gay' man and his homosexual orientation that never changed.

After extensive study, he discovered many truths in Biblical scripture that are not typically taught or believed in conservative churches. One of those truths is that the Bible does not condemn homosexuality. He has provided these truths in a clear, informative and user friendly format.

K. Darnell has served as a licensed minister in one of Los Angeles charismatic 'mega-churches', where he taught and ministered on various topics. He is currently working on his third book, a historic novel about African Americans in Los Angeles.

K. Darnell Giles holds a Bachelor's degree from a conservative Christian university in Los Angeles as well as a Master's degree in Human Behavior.

Table of Contents

Preface

Walk into any sizeable Los Angeles African American church for Sunday morning service and you will likely see someone who is homosexual, gay or Same Gender Loving (SGL). SGL is a term chosen by African Americans to identify themselves as having a homosexual orientation versus the term *gay* which for many serves as a reminder of the racism found to exist within the mainstream homosexual community. Although the term *gay* has been used to describe homosexuals in general, many Black SGL men and women have found themselves being marginalized among the *marginalized*. Black men and women use SGL as a designation of pride among those whose sexual orientation is homosexual. Throughout this book, I will use the terms gay, homosexual, same-sex attracted and Same Gender Loving (SGL) interchangeably, referring to individuals with a homosexual orientation.

Some may feel that I am making a generalization with this statement about gay church attendees, especially in light of the stereotyped image that many people have of the homosexual population. However, this demographic exists within the Christian church. What also exists is the large group of SGL men and women who do not appear to fit into any particular stereotype such as the butch woman or the femme man. You will find women who are delicate and beautiful sisters wearing Vera Wang Crepe mini dresses accented by Manolo Blahnik sandals with Austrian crystals, sporting African Twists pulled back in an attractive bun. You may find a ruggedly handsome brother with masculine and athletic appeal who looks like he could have worked as Ben Sherman's personal model when the suit the brother is wearing was designed. Why are these SGL men and women hiding in the sanctuary? They may not be. Sexuality is not a mantle that every homosexual man and woman wears. I choose not to wear my sexuality. However, we are a group who, while faithfully attending many a church service, can be and sometimes have been overlooked as viable and needed contributors to the church community. Oh sure, we will sing our highly anticipated solo and 'wreck the place' before the sermon, but our true identity must remain hidden. Why is this the case? On the surface, it appears that Same Gender Loving individuals do not fit within the structure of Christianity and its expression in the contemporary church. Homosexuality is a sin, right? When a few scriptures are read at face value, it appears to be so. However, if one takes a closer look, the appearance these scriptures give might be a bit misconstrued.

I believe African Americans, above all other people, owe it to themselves to take a deeper look at the scriptures for a clearer understanding of its teaching on homosexuality instead of passively continuing the marginalization of this people group. Most Christians who believe homosexuality is wrong, hold their position based on what they were told by someone else. A few scripture passages were pointed out (not studied) and their position was sealed. For hundreds of years, African American people have been oppressed as homosexuals are today, although in manners and with methods far more harsh. Our oppressors (speaking as an African American man) misinterpreted the same Bible to enslave our ancestors; and it is now used to marginalize and teach ignorance about homosexuals. The same holds true for how women have been treated in the distant and recent past within church culture and society as a whole. Women have been held back and not allowed to use their God-given gifts because the "privileged male" and the "privileged Christian" said so. Where do we as Christians get the idea that we (whatever group defines your 'we') are right and those who are *different* from us are wrong? Your immediate answer might be, 'the Bible'. My response in the form of a question would be, really? We (Christians) justify our 'correct' positions by 'slapping' an out-of-context Bible scripture on *our* belief, allowing us to denigrate the 'other', in word or deed, without applying Christ-likeness to our behavior. This astounds me. What is more astounding is that I have also behaved this way. Thus, it does not surprise me that many non-Christians do not want to have any contact with the Christian church or its members. There is a bumper sticker that makes an interesting assessment. "I love Jesus. It's His followers that I am afraid of."

I do not consider myself to be a Bible scholar, theologian or any of the like. However, I am definitely a student of the Word of God. I am an African American licensed minister who has been trained under several prolific Bible teachers and a well-known pastor in Los Angeles. I am a graduate of a conservative evangelical Christian university where I minored in Biblical Studies while earning my Bachelor's degree in Business. I also hold a Master's degree in Human Behavior. I identify myself as a regular person just like you, the reader. The research I conducted for this book was done on a level that any person with average intelligence could do. I read and studied the Bible in its original context and languages via dictionaries and lexicons. I also used online resources for biblical word translations. In my initial research, I purposefully did not use any traditional Bible commentaries, as I did not want anyone's opinion to influence what I would learn. I wanted to find out what the Bible would say to me regarding homosexuality, pro or con. After my study of the scriptures, I reviewed other books on the subject of *homosexuality and the Bible* written from a pro-gay and an anti-gay position. Two authors who are on opposite sides of the spectrum are Jack Rogers and Robert Gagnon. Rogers is a married, heterosexual Christian who coins his theology as pro-homosexual. He is a Professor of Theology Emeritus at San Francisco Theological Seminary and the author of many books, including "Jesus, The Bible and Homosexuality". Gagnon is an Associate Professor of New Testament at Pittsburgh Theological Seminary and is the author of *The Bible and Homosexual Practice*. On the opposite end of the spectrum, Professor Gagnon proclaims an anti-homosexual theology. I read these works to clarify the traditional positions from both sides of the debate regarding the validity of homosexuality within the context of the Christian church.

What I find shocking and disturbing on some level is the lack of African American ministers who have conducted biblical research and thus written on the subject of homosexuality. Many churches that are led by these men and women of God have quantifiable gay populations. In some of these congregations, homosexual members are more apparent than in other congregations. Living in Los Angeles and having been a member of a 'mega church', I can pretty much walk into any large church and identify the members who may be gay. I know the churches where it is known that homosexuals attend and/or are members. On one level, the membership and involvement of homosexuals is welcomed. On another level, remaining silent about their orientation is encouraged, if not demanded. Announcing that they have forsaken their 'former' homosexual orientation is applauded, regardless of their success in doing so. What I do not understand is why these ministers are not bringing an understanding of the truth about scripture surrounding this issue? I do know that a lack of education and resources is *not* the problem. The average person would be surprised at the number of people that hold advanced degrees in my former church. You would be equally surprised at the number of ministers and lay ministers who hold doctorate degrees. As I write, five African American men and women come to mind that hold theological doctorate degrees that I know personally!

For this reason, I feel challenged to embark on a quest for truth as it pertains to homosexuality and the Bible. I believe others need to take this journey as well. The status quo of accepting the literal interpretations that would suggest that homosexuality is a sin, in my opinion, is not responsible biblical interpretation and is inconsistent at best. If every Bible verse can be interpreted literally, than women should never teach in church and remain silent.[1] Actually, everyone should remain silent because the Bible tells us to do so when the Lord is in His Holy Temple.[2] I know this sounds silly to some and that I am "grasping for straws." However, this was my intention. It is a simple proof that the Bible must be studied and properly interpreted. I hope that other ministers will join me in this discovery and dissemination of truth, so that a population of people, who love God, will be encouraged to experience Him and know Him 'in Spirit and Truth'.

In this book, you will read of my experiences as a boy, a young Christian man and a minister where my sexual orientation has always been homosexual. The chapters written in italics mark my personal stories. I share these stories to give you a glimpse into the life of a boy who attempted to not see his life through the lens of homosexuality. I tried to be as 'normal' of a boy as I knew how. No pretense, just me. As a young man, I struggled for many years, eventually learning to suppress, hide and try to rid myself of same sex attractions and desires. I have hurt many people in the process including myself. In writing this book, I hope to clear up misconceptions about homosexuality and the Bible's position on it. The information found in the Endnotes section not only provides references, but informative notes as well. Be sure to read them. I must confess that the reason behind writing this book was self serving. I am a lover of God and His Word. I am fully confident in the love that God has for me, and the salvation I have in Him, even more so, now that I have embarked on this journey. I wrote this book from the research I conducted to understand for myself from scripture, if the God who loves me, actually condemns homosexuality. I have studied the Bible, applied sound hermeneutical principles, strained to understand the context of various passages and tried very hard not to read into any passage what is not there. Additionally, I have shared some experiences from the various development stages in my life. I was a pretty typical child who experienced some of the joys and pains that many other people have experienced. Needless to say, some pains were worse than others. I used to believe that those specific pains, like being molested, were the reason I 'became' homosexual. Although that tragedy caused other emotional challenges, I now understand it did not determine my sexual orientation. Some of the challenges that I faced were related to my self-esteem, my feelings of security and my overall gender self-concept. I have worked hard over the years to correct these misconceptions; yet my sexual orientation has consistently remained predominately homosexual and it is just as natural as my eye color.

I do not believe that there is not enough written in the Bible to adequately support God's design of homosexuals, but our existence is evidence that He did. There are many things and beings that exist in our society whose creation the Bible does not mention. The Bible mentions the existence of dogs, but not of cats. However, cats do exist. The domestication of cats is not mentioned, but we have both dogs and cats as household pets. Matthew 19 mentions that some eunuchs (emasculated or sexually incapacitated men) were 'born from their mother's womb', but does not mention creative intent nor defect. Then there are passages that have distinct homosexual overtones, but the information provided is not enough to definitively conclude homosexual relationships or activity.[3] Similarly, there is no clear biblical basis for the condemnation of homosexuality. I know this may be a hard pill to swallow for many, since conservative Christianity teaches otherwise. This truth will be uncovered in the pages of this book. In an attempt to be a little more tolerant, some Christian churches point to homosexual *activity* and define the *behavior* as sinful; not necessarily the person's orientation. Does this type of position mean the person is not homosexual if she does not engage in sexual activity, thus is not a sinner? If a heterosexual person is not sexually active, are they no longer heterosexual? Of course not. Sexuality is a part of a person's total being, if they are sexually active or not. Catholic priests take a vow of celibacy. Many of these men are heterosexual who have not and will never engage in heterosexual sexual activity. They are sexual beings with a sexual orientation. Sexual behavior cannot be divorced from sexual orientation; however sexual behavior is not a definition for sexual orientation.

Currently within the African American community, there are limited resources (if any at all) that speak to the issue of homosexuality and faith in a positive and balanced light. Although the truths in this book are ethnically universal, I attempt to fill the gap that resides in my community. I advise you to read this book with a Christian Bible near by, so that you can see for yourself, not simply what the words *say*, but what they actually *teach;* not the letter of the law, but the Spirit. If you are so inclined, you can also look up the various endnotes I referenced throughout the book to confirm various definitions and contexts as well. God, in His grace, has already revealed the truth. It is our responsibility to seek out that truth, if we so choose. Speaking as a minister, we have a greater responsibility to seek out the truth because we will be held accountable to correctly teach it. Once truth has been revealed, I pray that you will accept the responsibility of properly responding to the truth and sharing it as well.

My earnest desire is for the church and for society to lead the way in understanding, loving and accepting homosexually oriented people. No one with a desire to worship and serve God should be excluded. The church is not a building. It is a group of people who love, worship and serve God together. This group automatically includes heterosexuals and homosexuals, alike. May God bless you as you read and may God's Holy Spirit enlighten and love you into truth.

CHAPTER 1
From Gay to Straight to Gay Again

I have been attracted to guys for as long as I can remember. I wished that society and the church had room in their limited viewpoints and understanding of human sexuality to allow me to grow into "whoever" I would have become. But neither did. I do not say this as an indictment or criticism. It simply is a fact. I do not say this with regret as my life course allowed me to become the father of my beautiful children. I cannot say that, as a child, I experienced any extreme cruelty related to my sexuality. I was picked on and teased at times, but, as far as intensity and frequency goes, probably no more than any other kid. For this I am grateful. However, the names that I was called (like Kathy by my friends' older brother) and the negative inferences to my sexuality were quite painful. Growing up as an openly gay black youth was basically nonexistent in the 70s and 80s in Los Angeles. Neither my peers nor their parents would have allowed me to self-identify as Same-Gender-Loving (SGL) without opposition. The ridicule would have been unbearable. So I remained silent.

I have two memories as a child surrounding my sexuality and my friend's parents. One day my friend Antoine's mother took a bunch of us 'guys' to McDonalds for lunch. I was always fond of Antoine's parents. In my neighborhood, their parents resembled stability and love within a family. Antoine's dad never held back his affection from his sons. Antoine and his brother Derek were never embarrassed when their dad told them he loved them. He would even kiss them on the lips, in front of their friends when he would leave for work. It was obvious to me that the rest of us were missing out on a great relationship with our dads. By the way Antoine and Derek are both heterosexual. Three or four of us were piled in the backseat of his mom's new Chevy Monte Carlo as she drove. As usual, I was being picked on for not be masculine or good enough in sports or something. One of the other guys called me a sissy or a similar name and Antoine's mother spoke up in my defense. After correcting my friend's disrespectful comment, she stated that everyone is different, that I could not change who I was and that it was OK for me to be me. At the time, I didn't understand the validation she was giving 'me'. She was saying it was nothing wrong with being gay without using words that the other kids could use against me. I didn't have a clear understand or category for my sexuality at the time. I always wondered why I liked her so much. She accepted me unconditionally. Years later, I stood graveside at her funeral inconsolable with sobs and tears as I then understood that her unconditional love for me made such a life changing impact. I still think about her to this day.

Another memorable experience came from my friend Julius's father. When I was in junior high school, I was in the school band. I played the clarinet. Not viewed as the most 'masculine' instrument, I bore the brunt of ridicule, but I loved my horn! My closest buddies were all drummers (assumed to be a masculine instrument) and they also played for the school's drill team. A precursor to the movie, Drumline, they provided the 'beat' for all of the cute girls in short skirts which raised their level of cool, exponentially. I would hang out with them while they practiced after school and sometimes in Julius's backyard. One day while *they were practicing, his father came into the yard and told me to go get my "flute", an attempt to further* feminize *my instrument, so I could dance around in my panties and play while they practiced the drums! To this day, twenty five years later, it astounds me that a grown man could think his insult was an appropriate thing to say to a child. The pain of that moment is gone, but so has the respect for this man.*

Slavery, Jim Crow and ignorant comments like the one previously mentioned have done such damage to the psyche of African American men that we are afraid to show any sign of weakness. No one will take advantage of us again if we can help it. Sadly, our perception of weakness is skewed, as a man who fathers a child that he will never raise, wears as a badge of honor to some observers and is excused by others. "Well, you know…I can't raise my kids 'cause a brother can't get a break." Please understand that absentee fathers exist in every community and ethnicity, not just African American. However, responsibility may not come easy, but it is not impossible. No healthy able-bodied father should be absent from his child's life nor exempted from provisional responsibility. Irresponsibility is the true weakness. Conversely, two SGL Black men who are willing to adopt and raise children whose parents have thrown them away (or simply are unable to care for them), are also perceived as weak and less than men because they are same-sex attracted. There is nothing stronger than men who stand up and take responsibility in a situation that they did not create. I have learned the hard way of the damage that words and actions can cause and how the inability to retract them, can leave emotional scars that last for years, if not a lifetime.

As a young kid, I remember wanting to be physically close to boys, in a way I didn't want to be with girls. For as long as I can remember, I have had an attraction, a drawing toward males. I was very comfortable around girls; I could play and talk with them and relate emotionally in ways that seemed foreign to my male friends. As I entered puberty, my sexual attraction was exclusively towards guys. I really didn't have a desire to be with a girl sexually, outside of peer pressure. The rare occasions that I would approach a girl for sex was when I felt too much pressure from my male friends to do so. I would feel relief when some girl would thwart my advances because I was afraid of what the encounter would entail. What made things worse was I was already engaging in sexual activities with other boys.

In high school, I played in the marching band. It was one of the highlights of my life. Playing in marching band was my way of avoiding the pain of my growing, yet confusing sexuality as well as masking it from others. My clarinet playing and leadership skills earned me the spot of first chair in the woodwind section of the band. Later, I became one of the drum majors that led and directed the band. These promotions made suppressing my true self a little easier. During and after I graduated high school, I completely ignored my sexuality and faked living as a "straight" guy. I had a few girlfriends and they would have "put out" sexually, but I was too afraid to indulge, even though my older brother would encourage me to "get some." At the time, I didn't fully understand that I was gay. I understood the terms, "sissy" and "punk" to be a guy who was "scary" or afraid to defend himself. I knew that a "faggot" was a guy who liked other guys, but it was such a derogatory word, why would anyone use that term to describe themselves? I had been called a faggot before, but since I now developed stronger attractions to guys, I never wanted to be called that again. So, I made sure that no one knew of my attractions, no matter how out of my control they were.

There is a misconception that homosexual people have chosen their orientation and/or same sex attractions. In the Christian community, this is *based upon one's understanding of the scriptures, which appears to have no place for homosexuals. The Bible seemingly suggests that homosexuality is wrong largely because it is not a part of God's procreative plan. I agree. It is not. Since there are a few passages that seem to discourage homosexual behavior, it is believed that there cannot be a valid expression of homosexuality. There is no biblical text that overtly approves homosexuality. Since this is the case, it is believed that it is not possible for homosexuals to be born with same sex attractions. Therefore many Christians assume homosexual attractions must be a person's choice. There is no validity to this position and actually it is quite ludicrous. Homosexuals have no more power over the object of their sexual attractions than heterosexuals. Heterosexuals do not consciously choose to be attracted to the opposite sex. They just are. Attraction is not a behavior; it is a power…a property, similar to magnetism in metals. Two magnets do not act with each other to connect. There are properties within the metals that draw them to each other when they come in close enough contact. It is their orientation. This is how magnets respond to a set of circumstances. Sexual orientation is the same. A person responds to a set of innate genetic dispositions that draw them to the one to whom they are attracted. Similarly, school age children do not 'choose' to write with their left hand. It is their orientation to do so.*

Sexual attraction is not only about sex. There are many components that comprise attractiveness. There is physical attraction which is developed from how a person acts, looks, sounds and even smells. There is emotional attraction which basically is the intangible likeability of another person. Emotional attraction can lead to an emotional connectedness between two individuals. In dating circles, it is called chemistry. The foundation of this connection can be best described as affection. Affection is an expression of love that goes beyond friendship or goodwill and it grows over time. It is not restricted to romantic relationships, as affection is felt in a familial sense towards siblings, children and parents. Any individual who is engaged in a substantial romantic relationship will tell you that physical attraction may be what sparked an initial meeting, but an emotional connection is critical to anything that will last. When a person has a basic sexual attraction (which is different from sexual arousal) towards another person, physical, emotional and romantic attraction elements are what comprises this sexual attraction. These attractions are innate and natural.

After becoming a Christian, I never believed that a person could be born a homosexual. Prior to my Christian experience, it was not a concept that I had to reason with. As I write these words, it will be the first time that I acknowledge this truth to myself and the world. I was born a homosexual. Wow. As you read, you may wonder how I could have begun this informative work without acknowledging this simple fact. Well, my simple answer is this: the misinterpretation of biblical scripture that I learned, lead me to believe that being born gay was not possible. So, even after a reevaluation of the scripture and coming to the understanding that my sexual orientation is not the result of broken sexuality, I found it hard to believe.

As far as my expressed sexuality is concerned, I remained a heterosexual virgin until I was 20 years old. I was 13 when I had my first sexual encounter with a male and continued this activity through my teenaged years. Once I became an adult, I had a relationship with a woman for about 1 year. She was the first woman I had sex with, and I actually asked her to marry me at one point. I gave her a ring and proposed. Although I enjoyed the sexual part of the relationship (what 20 year old virgin wouldn't?), I didn't enjoy being with her. Eventually, I broke off the engagement and didn't date another woman for 8 years. During this period, I dated guys exclusively. Sometimes, my encounters were on the DL (down low - anonymous and secretive) and others were *relatively open. Eventually, I exposed myself to the gay community and felt a freedom of "being myself". As I met more guys like me, I felt less of an oddity. The fun and excitement of this new life lasted for a couple of years, until my faith caught up with my behavior. I was a born-again Christian. How I understood the Bible and what was being taught in church did not agree with my behavior. Although there were times I was in a committed relationship with one man, it was still unacceptable in the Christian community. After months of torment, I pursued an ex-gay ministry for assistance. Now, I am not one of those people who bash ex-gay ministries. I truly believe they are attempting a legitimate work based on their understanding of the Bible. I was involved with Desert Stream Ministry and commend them on the way they handled me and ushered me into a closer relationship with God. I have read stories where people said they felt like they had been brainwashed after their involvement, but I disagree. The difference with me is, no matter what anyone says to me, my faith in God is solid. I know and believe the Bible wholeheartedly and over the years I have tried to reconcile my faith and my sexuality. I have finally come to understand scripture better and do not have to put "the church", God, the Bible or anyone else in a negative light. Just like Jacob, I have wrestled with God in ways I would have never imagined, in order for me to allow Him to bless me. I will be forever grateful to and never let go of God.*

In addition to being a participant in ex-gay ministries, I developed and oversaw an ex-gay ministry. I have sought out Christian counselors to "overcome" my own homosexuality and must say that I respect my therapists as much today as I did then. They have impacted my life for the positive. My former pastor has treated me with nothing short of love and support through my homosexual "struggle". I am a blessed man. Typically, ex-gay ministries ascribed to a psychological model of reparative or conversion therapy to offer help to individuals with their issues of sexual and relational brokenness. Although, I agree that a lot of sexual and relational brokenness exists in both the heterosexual and homosexual communities, homosexual orientation is not a by-product of brokenness. There was a time that I believed it was. Currently, ex-gay organizations, like Exodus International are changing their position as it relates to homosexual conversion. For those homosexual individuals who have decided that living a heterosexual lifestyle is for them, my hat goes off to them. I wish them much success and happiness in their relationships. I believe Jesus said it best when referring to men who have decided to become *eunuchs (men who choose to not marry or father children), "He who is able to accept it, let him accept it."*

In an attempt to fix, reorient or heal what they believe is 'brokenness', reparative therapists and ex-gay ministries only address homosexual related behaviors rather than orientation. They do not believe that a person can have a healthy sexual orientation if they are attracted to the same gender, basically because the Bible does not appear to record it. There are many prohibited and allowed activities that the Bible does not record. The Bible's silence does not equal non-existence or condemnation of a person's homosexual orientation. The Old Testament scriptures prohibit and condemn adultery, at the same time, giving laws, which provide care and protection for additional wives and concubines. I have not once heard a sermon explaining this seeming contradiction. (I provide clarity on this contradiction in Chapter 9) The goal of reparative therapists and ex-gay ministries is to help the homosexual manage his sexual desires to the point they are no longer bothersome.

> "[People cannot] choose to have homosexual feelings anymore than heterosexuals can deny their impulse for the opposite sex. By acknowledging that 'reparative' or 'conversion' therapy is addressing only behavior rather than

orientation, opponents of homosexuality are actually admitting that, in fact, sexual orientation is a part of someone's nature and may be just as God-given as heterosexuality."[4]

"Sexual orientation is like handedness: Most people are one way, some are the other. A very few are truly ambidextrous."[5] *Although, many theories exist, there is no biological evidence that supports the cause of handedness. The majority of the population is right handed, just like the majority is heterosexual. A small percentage is truly left handed. Likewise, a small percentage of the population is gay. There are a few people who are ambidextrous, where they can perform tasks with either hand. There are a few people who are attracted to and are comfortable with having sex with either and/or both genders. There are theories for the causation of sexual orientation, but there is no proof for it. Is the cause as important as the reality? Not really. People just are. So now what should be done? One change to be made in society's mind is that homosexuals should not be compared to rapists and murderers in the context of biblical sin. Although, often heard in sermons, it is an offensive reference that carries no validity. Homosexuality cannot be equated to the hurtful and offensive acts of these criminals. At best, homosexuals would only be hurting themselves if sexual orientation were a detriment. As a society, we need to accept who and what people are and try to understand them as individuals and not put them in one big box. This is what drives bigotry. Every homosexually oriented person is different from the next, just like heterosexual people. This is proven by the amount of homosexuals who pass as heterosexuals, who receive love, appreciation and acceptance by mainstream society. They bring uniqueness to society and make positive contributions. God forbid these individuals acknowledge their sexual orientation. Then they 'become' these other entities that are ridiculed and shunned. This should not be.*

I no longer recommend ex-gay ministries or reparative therapy. I will not say that their work causes 'damage' to the individual because I did not have that experience. I have read about those who have suffered psychologically due to their ex-gay or reparative therapy experiences. I, personally, do not feel that I was let down by false hope as I believed in what they taught. They were not trying to 'convert' me; I was seeking help from them to become exclusively heterosexual. I have since discovered that this is not possible or necessary for me. I have friends that have participated in ex-gay ministries and reparative therapy. Some of these men were already married and remain married today. Others have decided to 'leave' homosexuality and have since become married and on the surface appear to be happy and satisfied. Others have remained homosexual as their orientation could not be changed. I am aware of one friend who is married and knows he is almost exclusively homosexually attracted. He has been married for many years and his sexual attraction towards his wife is almost non-existent. He holds strong to his beliefs and 'understanding' of the Bible and will continue to live a 'heterosexual' lifestyle. I love and respect him and he knows I wish him the best and hope his marriage lasts. However, he and I know that he only experiences sexual and relational satisfaction from the men whom he sees secretly.

After experiencing years of therapy, ministry, conferences, discipleship, and Biblical teaching on the subject of homosexuality, I also decided to get married. We had a challenging marriage, but a good one. God has allowed me to be a father to wonderful children who love me. After spending years making bad choices that I regret and hurting people that I love, I had to reevaluate my sexuality…again. I believed in the traditional biblical understanding of homosexuality. I embraced the belief as my own. I previously wrote a book on the subject of 'being delivered' from homosexuality. I have since discovered and acknowledged that my original position and understanding were both incorrect. I look to rectify this error within these pages.

What I have come to discover is that I am a man that is both gay and Christian. I can now say this without apology. I have no control over my sexual attractions to the same gender. My attractions are not my choice, sexual behavior and propriety are. I have already tried the "choose who you will be attracted to" thing. I tried to be attracted to women. Sexuality does not work that way. After 12 years of marriage, where I have hurt my family due to my homosexual infidelity, I am now divorced. As painful as it has been to leave my family unit, my acceptance of my sexual orientation has been the most truthful and liberating experience. I finally am truthful to myself about who I am. I do not blame anyone nor do I feel that anyone has held me back from anything. I am at the right place, at the right time. I do not endorse divorce or infidelity for anyone, heterosexual or homosexual. Divorce was the best option for our situation. It has been a painful and damaging process for everyone involved. My ex-wife, children and I have all experienced tear-filled sleepless nights due to the choices I have made. For us, this is now a fact of life. Our spiritual journey is not theoretical. It is painfully practical. It is my prayer that someone will benefit greatly from the challenges I have experienced and, on some level, caused.

The journey we will take in the coming pages will share some of my personal experiences, but mostly will be an evaluation of Old and New Testament texts in their original contexts from a clear hermeneutical (interpretative) perspective. The general task of hermeneutics is to seek the contemporary relevance of the Bible's ancient texts.[6] Discovering contemporary relevance of the biblical texts is the goal of this book as it has brought me liberty. The liberty that I now feel is tremendous. It is the liberty that Christ died to give me and I am glad that I am learning to see and embrace it. I am a man who is proud to be Christian, Black and gay. I don't say that in the sense that some do. I, personally, do not believe that homosexuality is a gift that should be celebrated anymore than heterosexuality is to be celebrated. Sexuality just is. I am proud in the sense that I am no longer ashamed of my sexual orientation. I don't have a reason to be. This freedom has allowed me to look back on my childhood and see how unique of an individual I was; how well liked I was by many and to see the great person I was and am becoming.

At 23 years old, I received a precious gift from my father on his deathbed. I suppressed the memory of it because it did not fit within the scope of my previous Christian thought. His gift was the following words.

> "Kevin, you are my son. You have always been my baby boy. I love you. I always have, I just didn't know how to show it. I knew you were gay since you were a little boy. Maybe 3 or 4 years old. I saw it then."

I asked him why he never said anything to me about it. He continued,

> "I didn't know what to say. I just thought that some people were born that way. You were my son. I loved you. It didn't matter."

When I 'came out' to my brother and sister, their sentiments were the same. I am their little brother. They love me and my sexuality does not matter. This book will not focus on the relationship I had with my dad while growing up. I will say that the relationship was not perfect. I had some fun times with my dad. Sadly, many were overshadowed by negative experiences and pain he caused, many of them unintentional. As a father myself, I clearly understand how we can fail our children. Had my father communicated to me that he knew that I was gay and that he loved me just the same, maybe my world would have been different up to this point. I do not know. Maybe I would not have had the opportunity to write this book. I am just glad to know that I was loved by my dad, am loved by my

Heavenly Father and that I have always been normal. I'm just me…and for those who know me, in spite of my flaws, I'm a pretty good guy.

Now it is time for me to continue to be the man God has called me to be at this stage in my life…a man who happens to be a gay Christian. Other Christians may cringe at this statement, wondering why God would use someone like me. He can, He is and He will continue to do so. There are many Christian denominations that understand the truths that will be revealed in this book. Their acceptance and inclusion of homosexual persons into the family of God is a great work that needs to be spread. God's gifts and callings are without repentance, meaning God doesn't change His mind in the manner that people do. He knew I would be gay before I knew who or what I was. This book is just one of the things He has called me to create. I am grateful and humbled at the task.

It is my belief that over many hundreds of years, various biblical scholars have used biased hermeneutical approaches when it comes to the subject of homosexuality. Interpretations have been given that have been framed in fear and ignorance. This book was written with the intention of destroying some of those fears by providing knowledge to the world that people with a homosexual orientation are just people, who are equally loved by God as any other.

Welcome to my life…my world.

C H A P T E R 2
In the Beginning, God...

The subject of homosexuality is as old as the Bible itself. In recent years, it has been the subject of many social debates, political campaigns and church splits. Many people show disdain for homosexuals and their relationships based on what they perceive the Bible teaches on this subject. Many of these opponents have not studied the Bible to see what it teaches for themselves, rather their belief is founded more upon historical church practice and rumors than actual facts. The issue at hand is *what does the Bible teach about homosexual orientation, homosexual behavior and homosexual relationships*? Our study will start at the beginning of the Bible with the account of creation. In addition to the traditional 'homosexual' scriptures, we will also look at the issues of marriage and adultery to see how they relate to homosexuality as well.

In the second chapter of Genesis, we find a more detailed account of Creation than that of Genesis chapter 1. In Genesis 1, mankind is created. In Genesis 2, man has already been created and then woman is created from the substance of the man. The two of them existed in a perfect garden before sin ever existed in the world. This account provides for us a pattern for heterosexual relationships and *possibly* a pattern for marriage. I say *possibly* because one example, albeit the first one, cannot be the sole indication of a pattern.

Heterosexual relationships are an essential part of God's plan for humanity. Only men and women can procreate, thus heterosexuality is critical and was purposed by God. However, does the context of the Bible teach that this essential part to God's plan is a requirement for every human being? Traditionally, this passage is used to validate that marriage can only be between a man and a woman. Thus, it is believed that heterosexual marriage is the only manner in which two people can form a loving relationship. In other words, homosexual relationships are in violation of God's plan. Some would even go so far to say that God **hates** homosexual people. I strongly disagree.

Together, we will look at the scriptures and interpret them contextually to determine the holistic message of the Bible as it relates to homosexuality; if there is a definitive message at all. There are approximately 11 passages that individuals quote to refer or elude to the subject of homosexuality. There is a heated debate between the "religious right" and "liberal left" as to what these passages mean and how they can be applied today. It is sad that these 11 or so passages have caused so much pain and discord, not only within the Christian community, but general society as well. The Church, the body of Christ, is to be a place of refuge, healing, restoration and most of all, love. So many homosexual people have experienced a lack of love from the church and society. Many people have been shunned by their families and literally kicked out of their homes when they have announced that they are homosexual. In such a sensitive situation, no one escapes unscathed, regardless to which side of the proverbial fence you belong. Parents, from a lack of understanding, react in damaging ways towards the children that they once loved. Children are rejected by those closest to them and learn not to trust others with their hearts.

Additionally, there are extremist groups who, sadly, misuse the name of God as they proclaim their hatred and God's *supposed* hatred for homosexuals. One of the most painful things to me is that God is so misrepresented in this debate. God is not a hater of people. God is LOVE. It may sound like a cliché, but it is an eternal and essential truth. God is love and he loves everyone. I searched the Bible to find where God declared that he hated someone and could not find one scripture. Proverbs 6:16, 19 says,

> "These six things the LORD hates… a false witness who speaks lies, and one who sows discord among brethren."

Even quoting this scripture is a stretch because the context of the passage and the Hebrew phrases reveals that God hates certain actions, not people. The same verse in the New Living Translation says, "God hates a mouth that lies under oath, [and] a troublemaker in the family." Instead of hatred, we need to exhibit healing, understanding, and Christian love, universally. However, this statement does not mean that all Christian people or Christian churches treat homosexuals poorly or have a negative opinion of them.

I have been a member of a church who tries hard to practice the equal and fair treatment of all people. I am a proud member of the Christian community. For many years, I was led by a pastor who is aware of my sexual orientation. He is not afraid to talk to me about homosexuality, even if we disagreed. He does not solely define me by my sexual orientation and he loves and respects me as a friend, a brother and as a Christian. His love and support of me is proof that not all Christians who disagree with homosexuality are filled with and teach hate.

I am a born-again Christian who is a licensed minister of the Gospel, so I have no intentions of bad mouthing my own people, thereby bad mouthing myself. What I intend to do is shed some light on the truth of what the Bible does and does not say about homosexuality. I will show that a doctrine on homosexuality cannot be developed from the handful of scriptures that are used to condemn it. Once ignorance is dispelled and accurate knowledge is obtained, then healing and acceptance can go forth for those who are homosexual. Love can be restored in families, communities and even in those churches that have lost it.

A major theme in the Bible is the practice of hospitality. The word hospitality means to entertain guests, visitors or strangers in a generous and friendly manner. The scriptures are full of references on how to treat your fellow man and the need for social justice. Jesus gave us these instructions. It is one of the greatest commandments,

> "You shall love the LORD your God with all your heart, with all your soul, with all your strength, and with all your mind,' and 'your *neighbor* as yourself."[7] [Italics mine]

How often is this practiced? Do we really treat our neighbor as well as we treat ourselves? Our neighbor would include that widowed or single mother who needs help with her children, the homeless man who needs a meal to eat, or the elderly man who no longer has the strength to mow his lawn. It also includes the lesbian couple next door who simply wants to live in a safe community like you. The list goes on; however, we are most often too busy to extend a loving and welcoming hand. I am not excluded. Here are 7 additional scriptures that mention the importance of hospitality: Romans 12:13, I Timothy 3:2, I Peter 4:9, Hebrews 13:2, 3 John 5-6, I Peter 4:9, Hebrews 13:2. This brief list does not even include passages from the Old Testament or the Gospels! Hospitality is a practice exampled by and commanded by God. Hospitality is a lifestyle choice.

Christians are to "bear the image" of God. This means that other people can 'see' God through the life we live. Our lives should be an obedient representation of the scriptures. For example, in looking at the plan of God for heterosexuality and bearing children, are all people capable of *bearing the image* of God in this way? Jesus addressed this Himself in Matthew 19:10-12. In this passage, Jesus was teaching on the subject of marriage and divorce, quoting from Genesis 2. After his lesson, he begins to talk about a group of people called eunuchs. Eunuchs were men who choose not to or were incapable of marrying and fathering children. For the men who were incapable of fathering children, Jesus offers no words of condemnation nor does He suggest that they need healing. He simply states that *these eunuchs were born from their mother's womb.* These men do not fit within the procreative plan of God; some by choice, others by birth. Others who do not fit in this plan are unhealed barren women. These are women who are unable to conceive and bear children. We have both of these types of men and women in our society today. Are these men and women to be cast away by

God because they are not bearing His image through procreation? Are they committing some type of sin because they cannot or choose not to produce children? Of course not.

Another part of God's divine plan is salvation for all people. Matthew 18:11 teaches that God's desire is for everyone to be saved. If 1% of a group is lost (unsaved), God will leave the 99% to find and bring back the 1%. It is not God's will that any person perish. However, throughout Jesus' earthly ministry, how many people were around, to whom He did **not** minister salvation? This number is not recorded. Physical healing is a part of God's will and plan. Isaiah 53 beautifully and prophetically describes a portion of Jesus' earthly ministry. A part of this description was quoted in I Peter 2:24. *By Jesus' stripes, we are healed*, which means that the abuse He endured on the cross, His death, burial and resurrection – the finished work of Christ – provides healing for us. Luke 4:18-27 records a time when Jesus went to the synagogue and read Isaiah 61 which states that God sent Him to heal the brokenhearted, set at liberty the captives and recover sight to the blind. Jesus was to continue God's ministry of physical healing, according to His heavenly Father's will. However, Luke 4:27 mentions that there were *many* unhealed lepers in Israel during Elijah's time. It has always been Jesus and God the Father's will to heal; however, like the Luke account teaches, some people are not. And we do not have the answer as to why.

John 5:1-9 gives an account of a lame man who was healed in Jerusalem.

John 5:1-9

After this there was a feast of the Jews, and Jesus went up to Jerusalem. ² Now there is in Jerusalem by the Sheep Gate a pool, which is called in Hebrew, Bethesda, having five porches. ³ In these lay a great multitude of sick people, blind, lame, paralyzed, waiting for the moving of the water. ⁴ For an angel went down at a certain time into the pool and stirred up the water; then whoever stepped in first, after the stirring of the water, was made well of whatever disease he had. ⁵ Now a certain man was there who had an infirmity thirty-eight years. ⁶ When Jesus saw him lying there, and knew that he already had been in that condition a long time, He said to him, "Do you want to be made well?" ⁷ The sick man answered Him, "Sir, I have no man to put me into the pool when the water is stirred up; but while I am coming, another steps down before me." ⁸ Jesus said to him, "Rise, take up your bed and walk." ⁹ And immediately the man was made well, took up his bed, and walked. And that day was the Sabbath.

There was a great crowd of all types of sick people. At a particular time, an angel of God would stir the water and whoever got in the water *first* would be healed. Is healing a part of God's plan? Yes. Does everyone receive healing? No. Jesus saw a man there who was sick for 38 years. He had been at the pool for a long time hoping to get healed. Jesus took it upon Himself to heal the man. Thank God. But how many people were not healed that day? Many people were not healed because after Jesus healed this particular man, the Bible says He left the pool *because of the crowd*. Maybe it was because He couldn't physically touch everybody. This is a possibility, but physical touch was not required of Jesus. There were plenty of times when he spoke words and a person was healed.

God's will does not always happen the way we understand or expect it. His pattern and plan is not an absolute for everyone. Many know this from practical experience. I, personally, lost both of my parents to cancer, all the while praying for their healing. Does their death invalidate the power and will of God? Not at all. All men and women will not be healed. All men and women will not be saved. All men and women will not get married. All men and women will not bear children. And all men and women are not heterosexual. We can find release from guilt, fear and bondage in the words of Jesus when He talks about the eunuchs. Some eunuchs were men born without the capacity to marry or father children. They did not fit into the Genesis 2 pattern of multiplying and filling the earth. Jesus neither condemned them nor healed them. It is clear that all people are not the same nor should we expect them to be. The pattern that all men should follow is that of Jesus Himself. Acceptance.

CHAPTER 3
Elementary School

In elementary school, recess and lunchtime were always hard for me. Sure, I enjoyed the break from schoolwork, even though I was a bookworm. My timidity and caution would rise when I had to play some type of sport or interact with the alpha male jock type of guys. I know. How much of an alpha male can an 11 year old be? In this respect, boys are like a litter of puppies. They fight and pick on each other until the dominant one rises to the top for the others to follow. I was not that guy, at eleven or any other age in my childhood. I remember Keith and Robert. These guys were the jocks. When it was time for team sports, they automatically became team captains. In elementary school, the sport you played during Physical Education would rotate throughout the year. Our teacher would announce the next sport would be 'sock ball' and kids would start yelling, "I'm on Keith's team." Keith was the strongest guy in our class and he could sock the ball from one end of the yard to the other. Who wouldn't want to be on his team? Keith was cool with me. I didn't get on his bad side and he gave me no trouble. But on some level, I wished that I could be in his world. I wished that I could be the kind of guy he was. A real guy's guy. Strong, athletic, confident. But I wasn't. I was the talkative, expressive, intuitive, emotional type of guy. I enjoyed running around and being physical, but I knew to stay in my element. I would not venture out into unfamiliar or dangerous territory. When it came to physical activity, I stuck to dodge ball, tetherball and handball. And of course, the monkey bars! But typically these were the activities for the girls. And when you hang around the girls too much, you get labeled. And so it happened. I was labeled a sissy. I hated being called a sissy. Sometimes I was just looked at like I was a sissy. Most times, I would try to ignore it. I learned to stay out of environments where the subject would come up.

I found that it was safe to hang out with boys who were a little quirky and out of the spot light. I begin to play with Milo and Eric. These guys were into Superheroes. Not just the typical Batman and Spiderman, but characters like Wolverine and the Green Lantern, who was one of the first Black superheroes. I was not into Superheroes; it just wasn't my thing. But I would hang out and watch Milo and Eric run around the school yard and play 'in character'. One day on the schoolyard, I began to notice someone. His name was Larry and he was an alpha type guy. He had a little group of guys who would follow him like waddling ducks. I do not know what it was about him that began to stand out, but he grabbed my attention. Larry was in my class and I saw him everyday. It was no big deal to see him on the yard. But this day was different. For some reason, I wanted to talk to him and be near him. I didn't quite understand it. I begin to play in the areas of the schoolyard where he would hang out. I would try to get in on the games he and his friends would play. That usually entailed playing tag or chasing some girls around the yard. I thought Larry was…I guess cute. At 11 years old, I didn't understand that I thought he was cute. Boys didn't look at other boys that way. I could not rationalize what I started feeling towards Larry, but I felt it. I liked him. I liked watching him. I didn't want to be him, but I enjoyed being around him. After weeks of hanging around each other, I tried to sneak up on him one day. His back was to me as I approached him. I moved slowly and crept up on him. My plan was to grab him from behind in a bear hold. Right before I reached him, he quickly spun around with a 'round house' kick. His foot landed dead square in the middle of my chest and I went flying backwards. I landed on the ground and every ounce of air in my lungs decided to go elsewhere. This was not good for an asthmatic boy like me. I squirmed on the ground, gasping for air. A crowd formed and eventually someone helped me up. Larry looked at me and said, 'Sorry man.', started to laugh and ran off with his friends. I had liked boys before, but Larry was the first "alpha" boy that I had an attraction to. I figured Larry didn't like me anymore and I never played with him again. Larry wasn't necessarily being malevolent. He responded the typical way an 11 year old would have.

My best friend in elementary school was Miles Williams. He was a cute short light skinned guy from a middle class family. He always dressed nicely in his cool clothes. It was the 70s, filled with bright colors, bold prints and stripes, tight pants and big belts. Miles was a ladies man. All the girls loved him and thought he was soooo cute. Rarely did the alphas or the jocks pick on him or call him sissy because he was the 'in' to the girls. Miles was my buddy. We became fast friends in kindergarten and remained that way all the way through sixth grade. Miles and I spent a lot of time together. We would talk on the phone all the time. My mother would ask, "What could you guys be talking about? You see each other at school everyday." We would talk about nothing. Just stupid kid stuff. My sister's best friend lived down the street from Miles, so she would take me over to his house to play on the weekends. The types of toys that Miles would play with were quite different than mine. I had the typical Tonka trucks and GI Joe action figures that I loved. There was a huge abandoned lot near my house that had a railroad track that ran through it. I would take my GI Joe action figures or Army men and play in the dirt near the tracks. I would always act out some type of adventure I saw on television. However, at Miles's house, his play was more expressive and relational. He would connect shoe boxes with string and pull his dolls and stuff animals around in the front yard. He had boy action figures but there were a few Barbie dolls in there too. I thought it was strange but no one said anything about it and I wanted to play, so I went along with it. We would dress them up in different outfits and play in a manner that girls would. Then our play would become aggressive in nature and we would blow up the train and kill all the action figures and dolls. It wasn't completely girlish, but it definitely was something that I would never do at home. There was a part of playing with dolls that I related to. This gave me the courage to sneak off and play with my other female friends in my neighborhood. I would hide out in Nicole's backyard and play dolls with her. I would go over to my friend Corinne's house, and 'play house' with her. I felt comfortable in this world of fantasy and the feminine. I didn't understand why, I just did. But I knew it was something I could never bring home. Deep down inside, I felt it was wrong.

Eventually, Miles's parents and my parents became comfortable enough with each other, where his mom would allow me to stay overnight. This would happen occasionally. They exposed me to new things. For instance, I had never been to a shopping mall. It was 1976 and they were shocked. His mom had driven 20 miles to Orange County to shop. It wasn't like there were malls in South Central Los Angeles. The Williams family attended a predominately white church in our neighborhood. You didn't see many white people in our neighborhood, so it was quite a shock to see so many. It was a Reformed Church and most of the members were Dutch. Everyone's last name was Van-this or VanDer-that. I had never been around so many white people in one place. They were nice people, and years later I found myself visiting their church during a spiritual discovery period. I would stay over Miles's on Saturday nights and we would go to church on Sunday mornings. I believe it was some sort of evangelistic outreach towards me on his mother's behalf. One Sunday morning, Miles and I did not go to church with his parents. I think we woke up late and didn't get ready on time, so they left us. We eventually got up, got dressed, ate breakfast and proceeded to play. Although playing with Miles was different than my playing at home, this day was even more different. Miles decided that Barbie was going to marry GI Joe. He set everything up and I served as his assistant. We played and the two of them 'got married'.

Then Miles said, "Let's play wedding."

"Who is going to be the wife?" I asked.

"I will." he answered. I didn't know what this game would entail but I was curious to see what Miles would do. He disappeared into his parent's bathroom and came out in his mother's nightgown!

"What do you think?" I didn't know what to think...or do. I played along. I was the husband. I had to carry him across the threshold. How did an 11 year old know about that custom? I remember dropping him. I don't recall everything we did that day, but I remember when he said it was time to kiss him. I had never kissed a boy before, but I did it. I 'pecked' him. Then he kissed me back with a long dry kiss. I didn't really know what to do, but I do remember that I didn't resist him. In some strange way, it felt pleasurable to be that close to him. Soon, we were interrupted by the sound of his parent's car pulling into the driveway. He scrambled to get out of his mother's nightgown while I sat guiltily on the couch. He came out just as their key entered the front door. We ran right past his parents, out the door to go play. We never mentioned what happened to anyone or even each other.

Miles and I lost touch after elementary school. We had a big fight right before graduation. He didn't like my new girlfriend, Tiara. He and my ex-girlfriend Lisa decided to get together and embarrass us. They gathered a big crowd around us and started to say some really mean things about Tiara. At first we just ignored them, but I felt I needed to do something to protect her honor. I stood up and told him to stop. "What are you going to do if I don't?" The challenge was out there and I was on the spot. Before I had thought about it, I punched him in the eye. I had never hit anyone before in my life. The power that I felt flooded my whole body. I didn't know how to fight though and figured I was going to get my butt kicked. I began to dance around and threaten Miles to do something. I knew if I kept moving and talking trash that the crowd would go wild. Every kid on the playground wants to see a fight. I wanted the crowd to cheer me on. I wanted a teacher to see the commotion and come save me. I don't know if Miles could have beaten me up. Probably not. I was too scared to find out though and just like clockwork, a teacher came and broke us up before either of us could throw another punch. We were taken to the principal's office. I don't remember what happened but I'm sure my mother was shocked to hear that her son was in trouble for fighting.

Miles and I didn't talk anymore after that. At graduation, our parents wondered why we didn't want to take pictures together. Our friendship wasn't the same after the fight. After graduation, we attended different junior high schools. Many years later, I would run into Miles at various church functions and concerts. We had long forgotten about our 'beef' and were glad to reconnect. By this point, I knew I was gay and would naturally wonder about Miles's sexuality. He appeared to be gay to me, but I would never ask him. He eventually married a girl from church, just as I had done. We have reconnected once again and have even had a conversation about sexuality. Homosexuality has not come up in conversation, but we look at each other and silently say, 'Are you remembering what I'm remembering?' I get the feeling that he is gay, but only time will tell...

CHAPTER 4
Biblical Interpretation

Before examining scripture to determine what it does and does not say, one must understand that the Bible was translated into English primarily from the Hebrew and Greek languages. Painstaking care is required for a reader of the Bible to, not only understand what the penned words and sentences mean today, but what they meant during their cultural period and to the people groups to whom they were originally written. Although the words have been translated into English, the words and sentences still need to be interpreted in order to gain full understanding and meaning of the biblical texts. All languages do not have corresponding or equivalent words for every term in every other language. For example, the way the word *love* is used in the American English language, does not exist in every other language. In most languages, two different words are used to describe the *love* for ice cream versus the *love* for a child. There are words and concepts that exist in modern language that did not exist in ancient times. What word from ancient Hebrew would translate to the word, "car"? In the absence of words or concepts, Bible translators do their best to use words that best fit a particular situation. In the case of car, some other 'transportation' word would be used to illustrate the point. Interpretation means to bring out a meaning, thus every reader of the Bible is an interpreter on some level. Every interpreter is subject to tools of the interpretation trade.

The Process of Interpretation

Two key tools in this process are called *Exegesis* and *Hermeneutics*. Exegesis means to analyze and interpret a passage of scripture. Hermeneutics is the set of rules that are followed when one is interpreting. Noted author and theologian, Charles Ryrie outlined some hermeneutical principles in his book, *Basic Theology*. The rules are: interpret grammatically, interpret contextually, compare scripture with scripture and recognize the progressiveness of revelation.

- To *interpret grammatically* is to study words and their relationship to each other. Exercising this principle will ensure that the words are being used and understood properly.

- To *interpret contextually* means to study the biblical verses based on other verses that precede and follow the verse being studied, as well as considering the theme of the book in which they reside.

- To *recognize the progressiveness of revelation* "means that in the process of revealing His message to man, God may add or even change in one era what He had given in another. "What God revealed as obligatory at one time may be rescinded at another (as the prohibition of eating pork, once

binding on God's people, now rescinded, I Timothy 4:3).
To fail to recognize this progressiveness in revelation will
raise irresolvable contradictions between passages if taken
literally."[8] Ryrie goes on to give several examples of
commands that changed with progressive revelation. (i.e.
The command of circumcision in Genesis 12:10 and its
profitability as shared in Galatians 5:2)

- When *comparing scripture with other scripture*, the
reader/interpreter cannot simply rely on the revelation of
the human interpretation of the book. All of the books of
the Bible make up the whole; thus the Bible is God's word,
not the word of the individual authors. The message being
conveyed is God's message. So, we need to know what
God's intention behind the message was. The human
author may not have fully understood his own penned
words or their implications for the reader. An example may
be found in First Corinthians 7. In this chapter, the Apostle
Paul was discussing the issue of marriage. He stated three
times that he was giving <u>his</u> opinion and not the Lord's
command on parts of this subject.[9] Paul's opinion came out
of his own experience with marriage. At the time of the
writing, Paul was unmarried. There is no biblical evidence
to prove that he was married at that time or any time before
his writings. However, Paul did have very strong opinions
about being married which are covered in this chapter.
Following is a review of some of his statements.

First Corinthians 7:1
"Now concerning the things of which you wrote to me: It is good for a man *not to touch a woman*." (Italics mine.)

The Greek word for underline touch is *haptomai* which means to have intercourse with or cohabitate with. Paul felt it best for men to not have sex with women. This was his opinion, not the law. However, we must consider how his statement has affected the psychosexual position that many Christians hold. This is a position on sex that Paul held in common with the church father, Saint Augustine.

First Corinthians 7:8-9
"But I say to the unmarried and to the widows: It is good for them if they remain *even as I am*; but if they cannot exercise self-control, let them marry. For it is better to marry than to burn with passion." (Italics mine.)

Paul indicates that the opposite of what he is, is married. He felt that the unmarried and widows should remain unmarried. This was a strong statement in a culture where women were marginalized and a large amount of their social status, provision and protection came from their husbands.

First Corinthians 7:28
"But even if you do marry, you have not sinned; and if a virgin marries, she has not sinned. Nevertheless such will have *trouble in the flesh*, but I would spare you." (Italics mine.)

Paul was emphasizing the pressure that marriage can bring when your attention is divided between serving the Lord and serving your spouse.

There is a term that is used in scripture to define a man who chooses to not marry. The term is eunuch. A eunuch (Gk. *Eunouchos*) is a man who is emasculated, naturally incapacitated or a man who voluntarily abstains from marriage. Jesus' words confirm this by his categorization of them in Matthew 19:12. Some eunuchs were 'so born from their mother's womb', some eunuchs were made of men (emasculation or castration), and some eunuchs made themselves eunuchs for the kingdom of heaven's sake. This latter category is where Paul fits. It is interesting to note what Jesus said about this last category, "He that is able to receive it, let *him* receive it.", reminding us that there are a select few individuals who can decide to and handle being unmarried and/or to abstain from sexual relations [Italics mine]. This was not a command from Jesus or Paul. Basically, Jesus says if you can handle singleness and abstinence than do so. Paul personally recommended abstinence. I go into further detail on the subject of eunuchs later in the book.

The Apostle Paul was the only apostle who did not walk with Jesus during his earthly ministry. Although he had the opportunity to meet the resurrected Christ, he did not have the privilege of seeing Him day to day, experiencing life issues from the perspective of Jesus and the other disciples. One must consider this point, when reading the opinions Paul stated in First Corinthians 7 on matters pertaining to marriage and thus homosexuality in the previous chapter. Some may consider this conjecture. However, had he been afforded the opportunity, might his stance on marriage and sexual relations been different? Additionally, Paul is the only New Testament writer who discussed the issue of "homosexuality", along with his strong opinion for Christians to remain unmarried. It begs the question if the whole of the Bible has a problem with homosexuality or if Paul had a problem with homosexuality at all.

The Goal of Interpretation

"The aim of good interpretation is simple: to get at the 'plain meaning of the text'."[10] Since every reader is automatically an interpreter, when reading a passage of text, "we tend to think that our understanding is the same thing as the Holy Spirit's or the human author's intent. However, we invariably bring to the text all that we are, with all of our experiences, culture, and prior understandings of words and ideas."[11] This is a key observation, especially in regards to issues that have or had long histories of misinterpretation, such as marriage, the role of women in society and ministry and the atrocity called American Slavery. Those individuals who used the Bible to validate slavery conveniently ignored the verse in Exodus 21:16 which says "He who kidnaps a man and sells him, or if he is found in his hand, shall surely be put to death." European men going to the west coast of Africa to take men, women and children for the sole purpose of trafficking them in their new found country undeniably fits this description. Sadly, the only people put to death during American Slavery were the enslaved Africans.

Throughout this book, I will point out how scripture has been interpreted through a lens of ignorance, as it pertains to homosexuality. How a Bible verse 'reads' is not always the same as what it 'means'. Throughout years of interpretation and the release of the 'new and improved' versions of the Bible, words have been used to connote concepts and definitions that did not even exist during the time of their original writing. It is critical for any student of the scriptures to study the Bible in its original context and not take the 'words on the page' at face value.

One major interpretation problem that presents itself is the difference between the English language and the Hebrew and Greek languages, as I mentioned before. Various words were translated into English and when a reader of the Bible comes across them, oftentimes they are defined or understood in their most common and contemporary usage. An example can be found with the way Paul used the word 'flesh'. Flesh can mean body in some cases (First Corinthians 15:50) and physical desires or urges in another (Romans 8:1). Proper interpretation is required in order to understand the writer's intention. Another example is found in First Corinthians 5:5 where Paul talks about the destruction of the flesh being a person's sinful nature, but it is often interpreted to mean destruction of the physical body - death.

Another concern lies with the modern day translators of the Bible. Since every person is an interpreter, it would seem difficult for the translators to exclude their experiences and personal beliefs when attempting to objectively translate the scriptures. If someone already has a belief about the meaning of a passage or word, it is probable that they will continue with that belief into newer or more modern translations without further investigation. Additionally, translators will take 'license' to translate Hebrew or Greek words into English words that *they* feel are most appropriate to describe their

Hebrew or Greek counterpart. One such example is found in the New King James Version of Second Timothy 2:17.

> "And their message will spread like *cancer*. Hymenaeus and Philetus are of this sort" [Italics mine]

The modern translators believed that the use of the word *cancer* would provide a clearer picture for how the false teachers' message was being promoted. The New King James Version of the Bible was published in 1982.[12] The term cancer would definitely provide a contemporary mental picture that readers could relate to. However, the Greek term that cancer is translated from is *gaggraina*. In previous Bible versions, this word is translated gangrene. Gangrene would have been a more common and recognizable disease in ancient times, due to the lack of antibiotic treatment. Currently, gangrene is more associated with diabetic patients and most modern readers would not create the same mental picture when reading this word as opposed to cancer, which is a more familiar disease. Is the use of cancer over gangrene an important translational issue? On the surface, it may not appear to be important. Cancer had not been discovered at the time the scripture was written, so the writer did not use it in his example. The use of the word cancer is not an 'error' in translation, as translation means to "make" something or to "present for consideration". The scholars decided in the NKJ version to not use 'transliteration" as was used in the King James Version. Using the word cancer, actually gives a better understanding of the effect of false doctrine. Cancer is a disease where an abnormal and uncontrolled growth of cells causes destruction of organs and body systems. Cancer cells are *living* cells. In order to treat cancer, you must *kill* the cancer cells. Gangrene is the exact opposite. It is a disease where cells have died usually due to a lack of blood flow to the area. The dead cells putrefy and kill adjacent cells and gangrene spreads. Early treatment for gangrene is revascularization which is a restoration of blood flow to the area. This process brings *life* back to the area. Although each of these diseases spread and cause damage to flesh, they are polar opposites in how they function. Thus, cancer gives a better word picture for the effect of false doctrine. In this case, the Bible translators used 'creative license' in accurately describing this scenario based on our contemporary understanding of how cancer and gangrene operate. The original New Testament writers did not have the medical knowledge that we have today, so they used the best analogy they could. This occurrence brings up a relevant point. Did the New Testament writers have a clear understanding of homosexuality which possibly prevented them from putting their thoughts into correct words? Paul used the word gangrene, but we see cancer is a 'better' *English* term to convey his thought. A translation team decided to change the word. Most readers of the Bible are even cognizant of the change. When Paul described what has become known to be homosexual activity in the books of Romans and First Corinthians, did he have the proper words at his disposal to clearly communicate his intent? Have the Bible translators over the last centuries misunderstood Paul's writings and the words he choose based upon their own opinions and beliefs about what homosexuality is?

The upcoming chapter "New Testament Homosexuality" discusses the books of Romans and First Corinthians. We will discover that some translation errors have been occurring for years throughout various Bible versions as it relates to usage of certain words that have been used to describe homosexuality.

The Responsibility of Ministers and Pastors/Teachers

As a licensed minister of the Gospel, I can speak on the responsibility that the clergy holds in the proper teaching of the Bible. The Bible itself clearly distinguishes the clergy's job. Ephesians 4:11-13 states that God gave gifts to the Christian body in the form of *people* (Evangelists, Pastors and Teachers) to prepare Christian believers for ministry work and to build up other Christians as a whole, in order to promote unity within the Christian faith. In order to teach, preach and prepare Christians in the Word of God, leaders are required to do more than *read* the Bible at face value. In depth study is paramount for correct understanding, teaching and application.

After Paul wrote this letter to the Ephesian church on unity and empowering the church body, he wrote letters to a young minister named Timothy. Paul instructed Timothy on such matters as doctrinal errors, pastoral responsibilities and qualifications of church leadership. In 2 Timothy 2:14-15, Paul tells Timothy to remind the leaders to not "battle about words because it is of no value and ruins the hearers." There was an obvious problem within the church where leaders were being irresponsible with teaching the Word of God. It seems that some leaders were trying to make some matters significant that probably were insignificant, resulting in a battle of words in front of those who they were teaching. Paul continued, "Do your best to present yourself to God as one approved, a workman who does not need to be ashamed and who correctly handles (or rightly divides) the word of truth."[13] To 'rightly divide' means to make *straight and smooth*, to teach the truth directly and correctly. Basically, leaders are responsible to help believers understand the truth about what the Bible is teaching by making a straight path to the truth. I have found that, where teaching on homosexuality is concerned, this process is not being performed.

Recently, I was listening to a teaching entitled "The Truth about Homosexuality" by Dr. John MacArthur, a well known senior pastor of a large church in the greater Los Angeles area. He serves as the president of The Master's College and Seminary and has authored many books including the MacArthur New Testament Commentary series and the MacArthur Study Bible. I downloaded this teaching from the internet which is a part of The Master's Seminary Faculty Lecture Series that MacArthur taught on January 29, 2008.[14] Because I am always in search of the truth, I wanted to listen to this well respected pastor's position on the subject. I must say that I was shocked as I listened to the lack of scholarship Pastor MacArthur provided on the subject. Before I continue, I must say that I do not intend nor would I ever attempt to disrespect Pastor MacArthur. I will say that I expected a more informed lesson from someone of his caliber, especially in light of the fact that his instruction was to his *seminary* faculty! Here are a few of the concerns I have with his teaching.

1. He made sweeping generalizations about homosexuals which makes me believe he does not have any relationships with homosexuals. Yet, Jesus was in relationships with 'sinners'. How else could he have shared the gospel with them, if he believes they are in sin?

    a. He stated that homosexuals average 500 sexual partners in their lifetime and half of them are strangers.

    b. He stated that homosexuals average 300 partners per year.
    (Note that these previous two statements are incongruent unless all homosexuals live for only two years.)

    c. According to Pastor MacArthur, these statistics came from the Los Angeles Police Department. He did not give a date for this statistical information. I doubt the LAPD has the time and resources to survey the homosexual community. These statistics, if true, most likely came from some homosexuals who have had some dealings with the police department which would be a biased sampling. These statistics do not represent any broad section of society, homosexual or otherwise. A true statistician would discard the survey.

2. The majority of his teaching came from scriptures in the Old Testament Law.

    a. He discussed the 'homosexual' prohibition from Leviticus 18:22 and 20:13. However, he did not mention that the purpose of the Old Testament

Law was given for the re-establishment of the nation of Israel. This law does not apply to modern day Christians in the manner that it applied to the nation of Israel, if at all. Jesus fulfilled the law.

b. In Deuteronomy 23:1, he equates all eunuchs to be modern day transsexuals. This is a little ridiculous since science and medicine of that day couldn't even conceive of a transsexual operation! Those men whose castration made them eunuchs did not have a chose in the matter, so they were not transsexuals.

c. He states that all eunuchs are an abomination to God. He never mentioned what Jesus said about the different types of eunuchs and His opinion of them in Matthew 19. Not only are eunuchs not modern day transsexuals, Jesus never condemned them.

3. In Acts 8, MacArthur, once again, misinterprets the term eunuch as a transsexual. Eunuchs were bedkeepers. They were servants who served the royal courts and it was thought to be a good practice for them to be castrated, so they would not be able to have sex with members of the harem or female royalty.

I only highlight these points regarding Pastor MacArthur's message because they are indicative of a large majority of teaching that comes from the Christian church about homosexuality. Instead of interpreting scripture to see what it has to teach us, preconceived beliefs are superimposed upon it, to make it say what someone already believes. This practice is called *eisegesis*. Eisegesis means 'reading into' the text what is already believed; or searching the Bible for scriptures that 'read' what is already believed, without a complete investigation of the text or context. Pastor MacArthur, like other pastors and scholars, may be a good and sound Bible teacher. However, as it pertains to his lesson about homosexuality, he has chosen not to use sound teaching and hermeneutical principles.

I am disappointed that leaders in the body of Christ, which I am a proud member of, refuse to take a serious look at biblical scriptures to understand that homosexuals are not sinners because of their sexual orientation. Some homosexual people may be guilty of sin due to their promiscuous behavior, but promiscuity is not relegated to, nor defined by, the homosexual community. Heterosexuals are just as promiscuous as homosexuals. Maybe if the statistics Pastor MacArthur quoted were taken from a heterosexually populated nightclub, we would see more similarities between the heterosexual and homosexual worlds.

Is there a reason why many religious leaders choose to not look deeper at the theological issue of homosexuality? Many of these leaders are seminary educated pastors and ministers. It is my opinion that some of them choose to not look deeper because when they discover the truth of what the scriptures teach, they will be responsible to make a decision. It is safer to remain ignorant; especially if they want to continue to be accepted among their religious peers.

The Word of God is a message of love and liberation. Unfortunately, it continues to be misused as a tool of division, casting homosexuals in a negative light and preventing individuals from this group from learning the truth about a God who loves them and wants a relationship with them. Hopefully a person's sexuality will, one day, be overlooked as a requirement of salvation and fellowship in the Christian Church.

CHAPTER 5
My Second Girlfriend

The relationship I had with my first girlfriend wasn't as interesting as the one with my second. Lisa, my first girlfriend, and I met in the fourth grade. We had always been friends in the normal way that elementary school kids have friendships. In sixth grade, things changed. We begin to see each other differently, and we begin to act differently. Her classroom desk was across from mine. I would catch her looking at me. She would do the same. I would pass her notes. She would smile as she would send back her answer. We would play 'footsy' under the table; innocently touching each other's feet. It was simple puppy love. It lasted about two weeks...

My relationship with Tiara was different. She was caramel in complexion with wavy dark brown hair. She was pretty with an infectious smile. Tiara was new to our school and my sixth grade class. She had transferred during the middle of the school year when her family moved into a house on my block. I noticed that Tiara would sit by herself most times during recess and lunch. We begin to talk and became fast friends. She was easy to talk to, unlike Lisa, who was very bossy, resulting in the end of our 'relationship'. It didn't take long before Tiara and I were 'boyfriend and girlfriend'. She had two brothers. Her brothers and I would climb trees and throw dirt rocks at each other on weekends. Tiara and I would see each other but we didn't spend a lot of time together on weekends. After all, we were only twelve years old.

I remember telling my mom about her. True to fashion, my mom became really excited. She became excited over anything that I did. But she would get especially excited whenever I talked about girls. This type of reaction actually carried on all the way through high school. I believe she was afraid to admit something to herself that she already knew was true about me. One day, my mother told me that a gentleman took ladies on dates. I understood the importance of being a gentleman. By this time, I was already carrying a handkerchief in my back pocket, as my father told me it was the proper thing to do. You know, in case I sneezed or something. I agreed with my mother and she set up the date. The next Saturday, my mother, Tiara and I were all on the RTD bus headed to our lunch date. My mother needed to chaperone us, so she shopped while Tiara and I had lunch at the K-Mart delicatessen! I was smartly dressed in a button up shirt and jeans. Tiara wore a nice dress. We shared a grilled cheese sandwich and a drink. I didn't want my mother to pay for my lunch date, so I used my own money. Tiara didn't seem to mind. I think she respected the fact that I wanted to pay for lunch myself. I would do this in the future as well, when Tiara and I shared a soda at Olvera Street on a school field trip. I emulated my father well. I was the quintessential 12 year old gentleman. I didn't always behave as a gentleman, however.

Being the well-mannered boy that I was, I always won the heart of my friend's parents. I was well spoken and quite responsible. Trusting me was a no-brainer. On Saturday, I was over to Tiara's house. We were talking about school and life and stuff. As we sat and talked, I reached over and began to play with her hair. I would rub it and stroke it while she talked. I placed my hand on her shoulder. She turned so her back faced me and I continued to rub her hair and she continued to talk. After a while, she figured out what I probably wanted from her.

"Do you want to go into my bedroom?" she asked.

"Sure." I responded and off we went.

We sat on Tiara's bed. We nervously stared into space. I begin to rub her hair again, but I would not look at her. Then she stood and took off her blouse. There she stood literally half-naked. I had never seen a girl's breasts before. It was a bit overwhelming. I felt suspended in time as I stared at her in silence. She turned and walked over to her vanity. She sat in the chair. She looked at me through the mirror and asked me if I wanted to touch them. I didn't answer her. I just walked over and cupped her from behind. It felt so nice, but it felt so strange. She began to comb her hair while I held her in a way that a 12 year old shouldn't. I released her and grabbed the comb. I begin to comb and rub her hair. As I combed her hair, she rattled on about something that I barely was listening to. My mind went another place. Our relationship had changed. The puppy love was gone. We had crossed a line that I didn't want to cross. Actually I didn't know the line existed. She thought that I wanted to touch her. Touch her in an intimate way. She availed herself to me because she thought that was what I wanted. All I wanted to do was simply play in her hair. So that is what I did. I rubbed, brushed, combed and played in her hair. As she talked, I combed it from one side to the other, then back again. I scattered little sloppy braids all over her head. She talked as if nothing had happened. She went on as normal…as if touching her breasts didn't happen. Combing her hair was better for both of us. She handed me a bobby pin. I pinned her bangs to the side. I didn't want to be her boyfriend anymore. I just wanted to be her friend…who simply was a boy.

CHAPTER 6
Old Testament Law and
New Testament Grace

Before we can understand what the Bible teaches about the subject of homosexuality, we must take a broader look at the Bible itself. The Bible has two major divisions: the Old Testament and the New Testament. Another word for testament is covenant. So, there is an Old Covenant or agreement and a new one. The Old Testament was an agreement between God and His chosen people, ancient Israel. The Old Testament chronicles the experiences of the Israelites from Creation to approximately 400 years before the birth of Jesus Christ, the Messiah. It contains the various government styles that ruled Israel from the initial theocracy where God Himself was the supreme ruler, to the judicial system where judges were appointed to serve as chief public officials for the people, to the royal monarchy where Saul became Israel's first king.

In the Old Testament book of Genesis, God established multiple covenants with His people, Israel. The primary covenant was established with Abraham. This agreement would be an everlasting one for all of Israel. God promised to make Abraham's name important and establish a powerful nation through him. This binding covenant was patterned after the 'suzerainty covenants'. In this type of covenantal relationship, a suzerain (overlord) guaranteed the weaker and dependent vassal (servant) certain benefits and protection. Out of loyalty, the vassal was obligated to keep the stipulations of the covenant. When the covenantal rules were broken, punishment was exacted based on what the covenant stipulated. [15]

Later in the Old Testament, God gave the nation of Israel a set of laws for which to live by. This Old Testament law contained commands, prohibitions, instructions and consequences which provided protection and benefits to the Israelites. The law was to help distinguish Israel from other nations, whose customs were not to be practiced by God's people. The law was to help keep them healthy and safe. There were all types of commands within the law. Some laws were dietary constraints. Deuteronomy 14:8 instructs the Israelites to not eat pork. This restriction was probably given to ensure the health of the Israelites. Food could not be preserved in their *desert environment* in the same manner it is preserved today, so the incidence of disease carried from animals to humans was quite high. Thus, certain foods were prohibited. Leviticus 19:19 gave instructions against cross pollinating seed and the prohibition of wearing garments with mixed fabric. Leviticus 19:28 forbids tattoos and piercings. Each of the aforementioned 'prohibitions' have been violated by contemporary Christians and the culture. Most people do not even give a second thought to their participation in these behaviors. Wearing e a wool blend suit is commonplace in our society, by both genders and gender specific clothing is completely relative and solely dependent on social trends. (Kilts would be considered a skirt in America, generally a female article of clothing)

Leviticus 19:15 instructed the Israelites to judge or treat their neighbors fairly; a law related to hospitality. Deuteronomy 6:5 commanded the Israelites to "Love the Lord your God with all your heart, soul and mind." This religious law was to ensure that the Israelites would not begin to worship any gods of the surrounding nations.

The Old Testament law was established as a guide for ancient Israel. Are modern day Christians required to obey or 'keep' it? And if not, what is the purpose of the law today? Remember the "law" is a part of the Old Covenant. This covenant was a binding agreement between God and ancient Israel for specific purposes. Ancient Israel no longer exists, thus the law does not apply to modern Christians as it applied to the Israelites. Modern Christians have a new and improved agreement with God. Within the Old Testament, there is a reference to this new covenant that God would establish with His people. Jeremiah 31:31-34 states:

> Behold, the days come, saith the LORD, that I will make a new covenant with the house of Israel, and with the house of Judah: Not according to the covenant that I made with their fathers in the day [that] I took them by the hand to bring them out of the land of Egypt; which my covenant they brake, although I was an husband unto them, saith the LORD: But this [shall be] the covenant that I will make with the house of Israel; After those days, saith the LORD, I will put my law in their inward parts, and write it in their hearts; and will be their God, and they shall be my people. And they shall teach no more every man his neighbor, and every man his brother, saying, Know the LORD: for they shall all know me, from the least of them unto the greatest of them, saith the LORD: for I will forgive their iniquity, and I will remember their sin no more.

God was planning to do something different. He was putting His law into the hearts of His people, so they would know Him in a personal way. He would forever forgive their sins and iniquities. He did this through Jesus Christ, the promised Messiah. In Matthew 5:17, Jesus stated that he didn't come to destroy the law, but to fulfill it. In Luke 22:20, He described the new covenant this way, *"This cup is the new covenant in my blood, which is poured out for you."* We now have a New Covenant (Testament) with God that is not based on the law and sacrificial system of the Old Testament. According to Hebrew 8:6, Jesus is *"the mediator of a <u>better</u> covenant, which was established upon better promises."* This new covenant is built on the shed blood of Jesus Christ. He was the ultimate sacrifice and no other sacrifice will ever be needed, *including your own.* Through Him, we have been eternally reconciled to God and our relationship with Him cannot be broken. In Galatians 3:24-25, we find the purpose of the law summarized,

> "Therefore the law was our tutor to bring us to
> Christ, that we might be justified by faith. But after
> faith has come, we are no longer under a tutor."[16]

This new covenant is not based on law, but grace. Grace is the undeserved gift that comes from God. *"For by grace are ye saved through faith."* (Eph 2:8)

How is grace displayed by Jesus in the New Testament? In John 9, Jesus encounters a man who was born blind. It was assumed, by Jesus' disciples (which was a common thought of the day), that either the man or his parents committed a sin in order for him to be suffering with blindness. Jesus addressed their concern about who sinned with this statement, "Neither this man nor his parents sinned, but that the works of God should be revealed in him."[17] Then Jesus healed him. Jesus encountered and offered grace to the blind man by healing him. He did the same for the sinner woman in John 4. In the passage, it is assumed that she was a prostitute. Jesus forgave her sin of prostitution and instructed her not to sin in that manner anymore. A quick analysis of these two accounts would show that the blind man's condition was inborn and out of his control. The prostitute, though her social choices may have been extremely limited, had more control over her circumstances. Jesus offered the same grace under these different circumstances. Contrary to popular opinion, Jesus extends the same grace to the homosexual Christian. You cannot study the whole Bible and conclude otherwise. There is a difference between the homosexual and the *blind man and sinner woman.* The difference is there is nothing wrong with the homosexual. Homosexuality is an orientation you are born with. It is not a defect. Having an attraction to the same sex is not a condition from which you need to be healed. The Bible no more condemns desiring the same sex than it condemns desiring one wife. We will discover this as we explore the Old and New Testament passages. It is interesting how the definition of biblical marriage is usually quoted from the Old Testament. However, the pattern of Old Testament marriage appears to be inconsistent. Scripture records that Adam and Noah each had only one wife. However, David and Solomon had multiple wives. God looked upon all four of these men with great favor and respect. However, scripture does not record God's condemnation of the latter two men for having multiple wives. God punished David for killing Uriah, Bathsheba's husband. 2 Samuel 11:27 records that the thing that "David had done displeased the Lord" was Uriah's murder and the <u>taking</u> of <u>his</u> wife. This was the first time that scripture records God's displeasure with him and David already had multiple wives at this time. Furthermore, when Nathan the prophet confronted David on his sin, Nathan prophesied for God by saying,

> "I gave your master's (Saul) house to you, and your *master's wives* into your arms. I gave you the house of Israel and Judah. And if all this had been too little, I would have given you even **more**."[18] [Bold and Italics mine]

Not only did God give Saul's house to David, but his **wives** too! He would have given David **more** if he had asked. We need to pause on this point. God gave Saul's wives to David! **God did this.** Does this statement not clarify God's approval of David having multiple wives? Yes, it does.

There was a time when God was also displeased with David's son, Solomon. However, His displeasure was because of Solomon's choice in women. He chose 'pagan' women who could possibly lead him away from the true living God, which is exactly what happened.[19] Why was the type of woman that Solomon married more important than the number of women? God was distinguishing His people from other people groups. The distinction is what was important to God. The number of wives was not the issue. Additionally, if the biblical pattern for marriage was solely monogamy, why did the law include commands regarding the fair treatment of additional wives and concubines? I discuss this in detail in the chapter on Marriage and Adultery. During Old Testament times, a man was allowed to have more than one wife and multiple concubines. Concubines were servants or slaves. Their job was to serve their owner in any way, which included providing sexual pleasure or the bearing of children. It is ironic that God never condemned Abraham for taking Hagar as an additional wife to Sarah.[20] Neither did God condemn David for having multiple wives. When a study is conducted on the subject of homosexuality, the subject of marriage and sexual expression within marriage needs to be considered. It is assumed that the Genesis 2 passage provides the only pattern for relationships in the Bible, but this is apparently not the case. David was a 'man after God's own heart'. This phrase means he was not idolatrous. He solely worshipped Jehovah God. And yet, he did not follow the pattern of Genesis 2. What David did, however, was break commandments found in Exodus 20:14, Deuteronomy 5:8 and Leviticus 20:10 by committing adultery with Bathsheba, where the punishment for both of them would be death. However, neither of them was put to death. So, something is not right. We either do not understand what adultery means, that the *supposed* pattern in Genesis 2 is not a requirement after all, or neither. The word adultery was sometimes used to describe the idolatrous behavior of Israel as noted in Jeremiah 3:8, but this description does not apply to David and Bathsheba. Regarding their adultery, there is too much left to question. A more accurate definition of adultery is when a man takes another man's wife. This was the case with David, Uriah and Bathsheba. One common thread found among the multiple marriages in the Old Testament is that of commitment. A man should not take on a wife, if he had no intention of caring for her. This prevented women from becoming destitute. Commitment was important to the heart of God. He expected men to remain committed to the women they chose. The Genesis 2 'pattern' did not apply in all Old Testament marriages in the way it has been traditionally taught. If the pattern of one man and one woman did not apply to heterosexuals, how can it be required of homosexuals?

Homosexual Orientation

Homosexual behavior and homosexual orientation are not synonymous. A behavior is an activity. It is something you do. Orientation is a position or a state of being. Orientation can be defined as an attraction or desire a person has where they may or may not have engaged in a specific behavior. We will learn that some aggressive and violent homosexual behavior was attempted by the men of Sodom in Genesis 19 and by the Israelites in Judges 19, but not all of these men were of a homosexual orientation. I would suggest that most were not, since both groups of men were offered women as a substitute for raping the men. In the Judges passage, the men *did* rape the woman offered to them, making it doubtful that they were all, if any, homosexually oriented. This account is also discussed in detail in the next chapter.

Some Christians, who believe homosexuality to be a sin, do not feel it is relevant to make a distinction between homosexual behavior and homosexual orientation. Others, who may understand the distinction, do not feel that acknowledging a person's orientation is important because a person's 'feelings' are not as important to

God as their obedience. They reduce homosexual orientation to being simply a person's feelings and motivations towards the same sex. Sexual orientation is more complex than this. However, these people believe the relevance of a person's feelings is not a significant part of the Bible's message. This concept must not have applied to the heterosexual men of the Old Testament! Dr. Robert Gagnon, author of *The Bible and Homosexual Practice*, is one of those scholars who seem to believe orientation is irrelevant.

> "The focus of [his] book on same-sex intercourse or homosexual practice, as opposed to homosexual orientation, is a reflection of the Bible's own relative disinterest toward motives or the origination of same-sex impulses. What matters is not what urges individuals feel but what they do with these urges, both in their fantasy life and in their concrete actions."[21]

It is interesting that Gagnon's opinion is so definitive and only applies within the context of homosexuality. Does the Bible's 'disinterest' towards urges and motivation apply to the polygamy of the Old Testament or heterosexuality in general? Gagnon criticizes a reviewer of his book, by comparing homosexuality to abusive and exploitive behaviors.

> "Would incest or adult-child sex or multiple-partner sexual unions be acceptable if a person could claim an "orientation" toward such behavior? [This reviewer] needs to get over his love affair with the concept of "sexual orientation" – a concept that means little more than the directedness of sexual desire at any given period in a person's life." [22]

What Gagnon fails to realize is the New Testament specifically condemns exploitive behaviors such as adult-child sex, which is different from homosexuality. Also, the Bible does not condemn multiple-partner sexual unions as evidenced by the multiple wives of David and other men.

Although Jesus spoke of marriage in Matthew 19, polygamy was still practiced from anywhere between 300 to 1,000 years after His death. Urges and motivations have always played a role in the life of the religious and non-religious. Saint Augustine, a church father from the 3rd and 4th centuries,

> "saw a conflict with Old Testament polygamy. He writes in *The Good of Marriage* (chapter 15) that, although it 'was lawful among the ancient fathers: whether it be lawful now also, I would not hastily pronounce. For there is not now necessity of begetting children, as there then was, when, even when wives bear children, it was allowed, in order to a more numerous posterity, to marry other wives in addition, which now is certainly not lawful.' He refrained from judging the patriarchs, but did not deduce from their practice the ongoing acceptability of polygamy. In chapter 7, he wrote, 'Now indeed in our time, and in keeping with Roman custom, it is no longer allowed to take another wife, so as to have more than one wife living.'" [23]

Augustine's conflict seems to be incongruent with Jesus' statement on marriage in Matthew 19. Who changed any laws or patterns regarding polygamy? Jesus did not mention the subject. All of the men of the New Testament era, just like the Old Testament, didn't think it was necessary to practice monogamy. It seems they were led by their urges and motivations. The New Testament, like the Old Testament, does not record any specific condemnations of the practice. Notice that Augustine's opinion was that polygamy was no longer necessary. I agree with his position, however, it is simply *my* opinion as well as it was *his* opinion. He also pointed out that polygamy was *lawful* among the ancient fathers (it was), but now

(New Testament era and beyond) it should not be practiced. It is unlawful in most contemporary societies and cannot be practiced.

Augustine made an interesting point in the previous quote on how society and Christianity arrived at our contemporary practice of marriage. "Now indeed in our time and in keeping with **Roman custom**…" Monogamy was a Roman custom, not a Hebrew custom. Monogamy was 'adopted' into Christian culture from its influence from Roman society. The Romans had a large impact on Christianity, both positive and negative. The Apostle Paul's concern with Greco-Roman influence on the church is clarified in his writings to the Romans and the Corinthians. A central theme in each of these letters was the influence of cultural idolatry upon the New Testament Christians. Men, up until the time of Augustine, obviously had not abandoned the practice of polygamy. Although the statement from Jesus in Matthew 19 sounds more like corrective instruction than a mandate, it did not stop any man's desire or practice towards having multiple women. The apparent desire for growing an immense family and wealth was a benefit of having multiple wives and concubines; but it was not the only benefit. It was not physically possible for all concubines to bear children for their husband-owners. If so, Solomon would have fathered at least 1,000 children by his 700 wives and 300 concubines. Thus, the fathering of children was not the sole reason for having multiple wives, additional concubines and female slaves. All of these women were available for sexual pleasure at any point. This was the benefit.

Furthermore, homosexuality cannot be compared to the vices of rape, incest, or pederasty (adult-child sex), as these are abusive and exploitive behaviors. Homosexual expression occurs between two consenting adults. Any person can turn any type of behavior into exploitation; however, homosexuality is not exploitive in and of itself. Many homosexual relationships are loving relationships based on commitment and mutual respect. Many heterosexual relationships are not. The number of 'fatherless' children in America provides evidence in this case.

I am not recommending the practice of polygamy. I am highlighting the extreme amount of attention that homosexuality receives as opposed to the limited amount of attention on scriptures related to polygamy. Scripture is full of accounts of men having multiple wives without God's condemnation and it goes relatively unmentioned. However, there are plenty of conversations about the 'sin' of homosexuality. How balanced of a conversation can this be? The answer to this question is in the proper understanding of marriage and adultery. Once these concepts are clearly understood, then we can look at the scriptures in proper context to determine, if homosexuality as we know it in our contemporary society, goes against the same scripture. Once homosexuality is accurately described in scripture, we must determine how critical it is to the Kingdom of God. Gagnon states,

> "If, as I show, Scripture opposes same-sex intercourse on the grounds that it is a wrongheaded attempt at sexual completion through merging with a sexual same, what difference does an orientation make?"[24]

It will make a huge difference. And who is Gagnon to state what a completed sexual act is? A sexual act is complete when the two parties involved are mutually satisfied. If Gagnon is referring to completed copulation acts for procreative purposes, than that is a different discussion. There is no proof in the Bible that same-sex sexual expression is 'a wrongheaded attempt at sexual completion.' As we will read in upcoming chapters, each passage that addresses "homosexuality" is actually addressing other specific activities that are in a broader context than sexual orientation.

Sexual orientation is a part of an individual's personal construct. If heterosexuals are not restricted from expressing their attraction to the opposite sex (which some church fathers thought should be restricted except for fathering children), then homosexuals should have the same opportunity, where scripture does not prohibit it. We will discover there is no clear scriptural prohibition to homosexual relationships.

This *new* covenant is for anyone who will accept it. The Old Covenant is not the Christians' covenant and we are not obligated to obey it. However, it is not to be discarded. It records the history of Israel and the actual covenant that Jesus fulfilled. It serves as the backdrop for Christianity and is a historical point of reference and a guide. Although the Old Covenant no longer obligates us, upon close study, we will find that Jesus has reinstated some of its laws. "Love the Lord your God with all of your heart, mind and soul" from Deuteronomy 6 was reinstated by Jesus in Matthew 22. "Love your neighbor as yourself" was also reinstated in Matthew 22 and revamped with Jesus' instruction in Matthew 5:44 to "Love your enemies." Christians are bound by a new covenant with God whereby *grace* and the redeeming blood that Jesus shed is the foundation. This leaves us with a question. Does the Bible condemn homosexuality in the Old Testament? If it does, how does that apply to modern day Christians?

CHAPTER 7
Old Testament Homosexuality

Does the Bible really condemn homosexuality in the Old Testament? The term 'homosexuality' is a modern term. Its origin is from around 1890. The classification of people called homosexuals did not exist during Old Testament times. This does not mean that same sex orientation and behaviors did not exist, as they did. It means when we read the Bible, we cannot superimpose current cultural understandings and definitions upon the context of ancient times. We have to search for the <u>definition</u> of homosexual orientation and behavior, relevant to ancient Mediterranean times, to determine what the Bible teaches about it. There are four central Old Testament passages that are referred to when the subject of homosexuality arises. They are Genesis 19, Judges 19 and Leviticus 18:22 and Leviticus 20:13.

<u>Genesis 19</u>

Historically, the Genesis 19 passage has been used to show the 'perversion' of homosexual activity. It is no secret that this passage of scripture contains descriptions of intended acts that can be classified as perverse and even homosexual in nature. The remaining verses in this chapter details God's anger at the residents of this town and the subsequent punishment for their intended actions as well as previous actions that are implied. What needs to be pointed out is that chapter 19 is a continuation of a conversation God had with Abraham in the previous chapter. A popular Jewish law is "Love your neighbor as yourself." In the Jewish culture, the laws of hospitality and the kind treatment of strangers were paramount. This is evidence in Abraham's reaction to three strangers that appeared at this tent.

In evangelical and fundamental Christian circles, the word *hospitality* becomes a hot topic when used in conjunction with homosexuality. This group generally believes that 'gay theology' has replaced the 'true' subject of the Sodom and Gomorrah story (homosexuality) with a different theme (hospitality). If the word hospitality truly means to entertain guests, visitors or strangers in a generous and friendly manner, hospitality is clearly the subject matter in both Genesis 18 and Genesis 19.

Genesis 18

Then the LORD appeared to him by the terebinth trees of Mamre, as he was sitting in the tent door in the heat of the day. So he lifted his eyes and looked, and behold, three men were standing by him; and when he saw *them,* he ran from the tent door to meet them, and bowed himself to the ground, and said, "My Lord, if I have now found favor in Your sight, do not pass on by Your servant. Please let a little water be brought, and wash your feet, and rest yourselves under the tree. And I will bring a morsel of bread, that you may refresh your hearts. After that you may pass by, inasmuch as you have come to your servant."
They said, "Do as you have said." So Abraham hurried into the tent to Sarah and said, "Quickly, make ready three measures of fine meal; knead *it* and make cakes." And

Abraham ran to the herd, took a tender and good calf, gave *it* to a young man, and he hastened to prepare it. So he took butter and milk and the calf which he had prepared, and set *it* before them; and he stood by them under the tree as they ate.

When Abraham saw the men, his response was almost frantic as he hurried to meet them. As was the Hebrew custom, he offered these strangers water to wash their feet and food to restore their energy after their long travels. Abraham had Sarah, his wife, to quickly prepare a meal for their guests. Genesis 18:1-8 is an example of how proper Hebrew or Jewish hospitality looked. It was also an object lesson that God allowed Abraham and Sarah to be a part of, especially since God pronounced His blessing upon them that they would conceive a child in their old age. The level of hospitality shown by Abraham was what God wanted him to teach his children and the nation that would come from his loins.[25] God had a strong desire for the Israelites to 'do righteousness and justice'. Once this precept was established, God immediately referenced the sin (or outcry) of Sodom and Gomorrah. God said their sin was very grievous. Here is the key. God said, in verse 21, that He would go down and see for Himself what was going on in Sodom. Enter Genesis 19.

Genesis 19

Now the two angels came to Sodom in the evening, and Lot was sitting in the gate of Sodom. When Lot saw *them,* he rose to meet them, and he bowed himself with his face toward the ground. And he said, "Here now, my lords, please turn in to your servant's house and spend the night, and wash your feet; then you may rise early and go on your way."
And they said, "No, but we will spend the night in the open square."

But he insisted strongly; so they turned in to him and entered his house. Then he made them a feast, and baked unleavened bread, and they ate.

Now before they lay down, the men of the city, the men of Sodom, both old and young, all the people from every quarter, surrounded the house. And they called to Lot and said to him, "Where are the men who came to you tonight? Bring them out to us that we may know them *carnally.*"

So Lot went out to them through the doorway, shut the door behind him, and said, "Please, my brethren, do not do so wickedly! See now, I have two daughters who have not known a man; please, let me bring them out to you, and you may do to them as you wish; only do nothing to these men, since this is the reason they have come under the shadow of my roof." And they said, "Stand back!" Then they said, "This one came in to stay *here,* and he keeps acting as a judge; now we will deal worse with you than with them." So they pressed hard against the man Lot, and came near to break down the door. But the men reached out their hands and pulled Lot into the house with them, and shut the door. And they struck the men who *were* at the doorway of the house with blindness, both small and great, so that they became weary *trying* to find the door.

In this chapter, the same two angels that appeared in chapter 18 arrived in Sodom and met Abraham's nephew, Lot at the gate of the city. At the end of chapter 18, Abraham tried to convince God not to destroy Sodom because his nephew lived there. He hoped God would spare the city because Lot was one of God's own people – an Israelite, one who God deemed righteous. God's angels were there to investigate and serve as an eyewitness to whatever the sins were, which is not mentioned in the passage. (However the sins are clearly mentioned in Ezekiel 16:49)

Lot, like the custom of his uncle Abraham, extended a hospitable greeting to these strangers by offering shelter and water for their feet. Then the angels opted to sleep in the open square of the city. Why would they do this? They were on an assignment. They knew that the residents of this city would show their true selves by the way they treated strangers. Genesis 18:3 says that Lot strongly insisted that they lodge with his family. His offer may have been extended for one of two reasons.

1. Lot was insistent on keeping the custom of hospitality and dare not allow these guests to sleep outside when they could be comfortable in his home.

2. Since Lot lived among the people of Sodom, he was aware of their behavior and feared for the personal safety of the strangers. This passage does not explicitly say so, but historical writings show that the residents of Sodom were known to mistreat visitors and sojourners.

The New Testament book of Second Peter 2:8 says that Lot was tormented day by day, *seeing* and *hearing* the lawless deeds of the Sodomites. This is why God said there was an "outcry" against them. The Hebrew word for "outcry" is za'aq which is similar to the word used in Genesis 4 when Cain murdered Abel. *After* Abel was dead, his blood cried out (tsa'aq) to God from the ground. Whatever the case, Lot was rightfully concerned. This account continues in Genesis 19:4-7, as the men of Sodom surround Lot's house and demand that the visitors be sent out, so the men (plural) of Sodom could know them sexually. This is where biblical interpretation of this passage has become misconstrued. Two phrases that need our focus is "all the people" in verse 4 and the word "know" in verse 5.

Verse 4 says that the men of Sodom and *all the people* from every quarter surrounded the house. These were two distinct groups: men and people. The Hebrew word for men is *enowsh* (which means men, collectively) and the word for people is *am* (meaning nation, people or kindred). Traditionally, this account is understood to have been men only. If this is true, why would the writer of Genesis mention the word *men* twice if both of these Hebrew terms were referring to men? The writer did not mention the same term twice. If, for some strange reason, the word was intentionally mentioned twice, why use two different terms to describe the same concept? Although, the men of Sodom are identified (because they were going to commit the rape), the *people* were identified distinctly and additionally. People would have included women and possibly, children, as to distinguish them from the men of Sodom.[26] The community of Sodom was not just a group of savage homosexual men. Although definitely wicked, they were people, both genders, all ages. There were families in Sodom. If the men of Sodom were all homosexuals, why didn't Lot offer his sons-in-law to the men? Of course, the social hierarchy of the day rated women and slaves as the most inferior, and Lot was in a desperate position. Also, there is no indication that Lot's sons-in-law had any other interaction with the men of Sodom, homosexual or otherwise.

The Hebrew word for "know" is *yada*. *Yada* has multiple connotations, just like the English word 'love' does. Yada means to know someone, to perceive something, to distinguish something or someone, to recognize, acknowledge or become acquainted with someone. On a few occasions, it means to know someone intimately or have sex with someone. With such varied definitions, translating the word by itself can cause great misunderstanding. Therefore, the word *yada* must be defined within the context of the passage in which it resides. Since chapters 18 and 19 are one large story and its context is hospitality, it makes sense that *yada* could be translated as "to acknowledge or to become acquainted with." If the men of Sodom were following the Hebrew custom of hospitality, then it would be appropriate for them to become acquainted with the guests, in the same way as Lot. This would not have been too foreign of a concept for the Sodomites, since Lot was sitting at the gate of the city when the visitors arrived. Maybe Lot sat there often, where the Sodomites could see his acts of hospitality.

However, the overall context of this passage suggests otherwise as indicated by Lot's persuasion of the Sodomite men in verse 7, asking them "do not do so wickedly". It is quite doubtful that the Sodomites were emulating Lot's acts of hospitality. However, it does not mean that they had not been observing him. I might add that their observation of Lot was contemptuous, for when Lot asked them not to do this wicked thing, the men of Sodom said, "This one came in as a foreigner and he keeps judging us." It does not sound like the men of Sodom were fond of Lot. Moreover, they wanted Lot to stay in "his place". They threatened him by saying, "We will deal worse with you than with them." Based on this information, the Hebrew word *yada* (to know) is not solely being used in a context of hospitality, nor does it suggest that the men of Sodom wanted to become acquainted with the visitors. *Yada* is being used in the context of sex and hospitality. However, given the threat lodged at Lot, the intentions behind their behavior was definitely violent.

Other Near East Cultures

In the previous chapter on Old Testament law, we discovered one of the reasons the law was given was to distinguish God's people, Israel from the customs and practices of neighboring nations. In the ancient Near East region of Mesopotamia, homosexual behavior occurred and is recorded in their history. Incidences of homosexual behavior were sometimes a result of establishing social status and hierarchy. One social practice occurred when a man of superior social status would anally penetrate a socially inferior man. This practice was an act of disrespect and humbling of the inferior man. In social circles, a man would not want to be equated with a woman and being the victim of sexual domination would do just that. Equating a man with a woman is undesirable today. Two popular but derogatory insults currently used are to call someone a "Bitch" (feminization through comparison to a dog) and to say to someone "Fuck You" (a statement of sexual domination and penetration). Additionally, in ancient war times, victors of a battle would rape the defeated male opponents. There was a widespread ancient belief that a male, who was sexually penetrated, especially by force, would lose his manhood, exempting him from serving as a warrior or ruler. The phrase, "rape and pillage" is common as it relates to wars and conquests. In some ancient cultures, extending the act of rape to male victims was the ultimate act of humiliation.[27]

I digressed into this synopsis of Mesopotamian history to draw an inference to the incident of Sodom. These men obviously desired to rape these visitors. The question is, why? It is unclear from the passage; however the location of Sodom was just a couple of hundred miles from the Mesopotamian region. Homosexual rape could have been a practice ingrained in the social fabric of Sodom. If so, it confirms what Lot witnessed based on a Second Peter 2:8 passage,

> "(for that righteous man, dwelling among them, tormented his righteous soul from day to day by seeing and hearing their lawless deeds)"

In Genesis 19:5, the men of Sodom used the term *yada* to describe what they wanted to do to the visitors. They wanted to engage in a forceful, non-consenting sexual act with these men, but they did not say so in those terms. They used the same word used when the first sexual experience is recorded in the Bible. In Genesis 4:1, scripture records that Adam knew (yada) his wife, Eve and she conceived. This was not the intention of the Sodomite men. They used the word *yada* in a euphemistic fashion. It was a sort of play on words; a double entendre. You can almost hear their laughter and see their sneers as they yelled out to Lot, "send those guys out here, so we can…heh, heh, heh… *know* them." This is not conjecture or eisegesis. Yada is a term used for sexual intercourse. It is not a violent term. However, we know the Sodomites intended violence based on their threatening statements. It is obvious that *yada* was used euphemistically.

Clearly, the men of Sodom intended on homosexually raping the angels who were visiting Lot. However, does that mean these men were homosexual, that Sodom was a homosexual community or that homosexuality was being referenced as the sin? No, it does not. Before looking at the Sodomite men, let's look at the definition of rape. Rape is any act of sexual intercourse that is forced upon a person.[28]   Rape, be it heterosexual or homosexual, is not synonymous with sex, sexual orientation or sexual relationships. Although sexual intercourse is involved, it is not an act of sexual expression. Rape is an act of violence that is rooted in control and degradation. Sexuality is just the vehicle used as a means to an end - degradation. Could some of the men of Sodom been homosexual? Of course. Just like in any other society, some people are / will be homosexual. Genesis 19:8 sheds some light on the sexual makeup of this group of men. This was Lot's response to the men demanding for the visitors to be released to them:

> "Look, I have two daughters who have never slept with a man. Let me bring them out to you, and you can do what you like with them. But don't do anything to these men, for they have come under the <u>protection</u> of my roof."[29]

This was Lot's offer to the men who had his house surrounded. Lot did not appear to be unclear about the motivation of the men of Sodom. He was <u>protecting</u> his visitors. If the mob was a group of sex-starved *homosexual* men, as some traditions teach, why would Lot offer women to a group of homosexual men? It would not be a logical response. Actually, Lot's response was not the best because he was subjecting his own daughters to a dangerous mob. We will learn later in this book that when a similar event took place in another section of the Bible, the outcome was fatal. In the culture of the time, a woman's ranking in society and in their household was very low. The value of wives and daughters was more on par with property and slaves in comparison to men. Lot felt that he was upholding the Hebrew custom of hospitality by protecting his visitors. Actually, it was Lot's personal responsibility and he would have done anything in his power to protect them. So it begs the question, if the Sodomite men were homosexual, why didn't Lot (a man) offer himself to the mob, in order to protect his visitors? Because he did not do so, does it mean he was selfish or more concerned about self-preservation? Not necessarily. Lot also had sons-in-law. There is no indication that they were homosexually assaulted. Lot did not offer them to the crowd, either. What it means is the men of Sodom were not looking for a homosexual experience. In verse 9, they told Lot to get out of the way or they were going to do worse to him than his visitors. They definitely could have taken Lot if they wanted him, especially when he went outside alone with the crowd and shut the door behind himself. They could have taken his sons-in-law. The crowd didn't even mention *these* men. In the New Testament, First Peter 2:7 describes the deeds of the men of Sodom as "filthy conduct". The Greek word for filthy conduct is *aselgeia* which can also be translated lewdness. It means total debauchery, unashamed indecency, unbridled lust, unrestrained depravity. The New Spirit Filled Life Bible says the men had an insolent defiance of public opinion and would sin in broad daylight with arrogance and contempt.[30] This verse, however, does not describe the sin of Sodom to be homosexuality, in behavior or orientation. Furthermore, this account is not a definition for homosexual behavior in general. The intention of the Sodomites was not to engage in homosexual relations; it was to commit rape, a pure violent act. Their goal was to degrade these visitors and humiliate Lot. It was a violence that they paid for with their lives.

A summary of chapters 18 & 19 shows that the sin for which God judged Sodom was an abusive lack of hospitality. There is no scripture outside of the Genesis passage that directly refers to homosexuality when referring to Sodom. A homosexual context is automatically read in because the text is approached eisegetically. The reader wants the other texts to refer to homosexuality, so for him it does. The only problem is the interpretation is not correct. The prophet Ezekiel clarifies the intentions and mindset of the people of Sodom. The Sodomites were "arrogant, overfed and unconcerned; they did not help the poor and needy."[31] How is it that this clear explanation is so often ignored? This inhospitable position has been collaborated in the New Testament by Jesus[32] himself as well as in other early Christian writings outside of the Bible such as the following quote from the book of First Clement 11:1:

> "By hospitality and goodness Lot was saved out of
> Sodom when the whole region round about was
> judged with fire and brimstone; the Lord making it
> manifest that he leaveth not them that hope upon
> him, but appointeth to punishment and torment
> them that turn in another way."

Clement acknowledges that it was hospitality and goodness that saved Lot out of Sodom. If the main sin of Sodom was homosexuality, why did Clement not mention that Lot's abstinence from homosexuality saved him? Why did he focus on their lack of hospitality and goodness? The correct issue of concern is discussed and it was not homosexuality. The Jewish historian, Josephus understood the violent nature of the Sodomites as well. He makes reference to the encounter with the angels.

> "But the Sodomites, on seeing these young men of remarkable fair appearance whom Lot had taken under his roof, were bent only on <u>violence</u> and <u>outrage</u> to their youthful beauty." [33]

Josephus' commentary puts the climate of Sodom in perspective. If the men of Sodom envied the 'beauty' of the men (angels), their attempt at anal rape would be a means to emasculate and humiliate them. Again, Sodom's crime was an attempted violent attack, which obviously violated any rule or practice of hospitality.

Judges 19-20: The Long Lost Passage

This account in Judges is very similar to the Sodom and Gomorrah story in Genesis 19. The Judges passage chronicles *another* episode of atrocious inhospitality in the time of ancient Israel. The difference between the Judges passage and the Genesis passage is the perpetrators of the Judges crime were *Israelites* – God's chosen people! The story is as follows...

There was a Hebrew man, a Levite who had taken for himself a concubine.[34] (Customarily, a man had this type of concubine for purposes of sexual pleasure. The other type of concubine, Ishshah, had wife-like duties such as keeping the household and bearing children.) While returning from the house of the concubine's father, the man's servant asked to lodge with the Jebusites. The Levite refused because he didn't want to lodge in a foreign land. He wanted to lodge with fellow Israelites, so they traveled on to Gibeah, which was a part of the

Israelite tribe of Benjamin. When he arrived in Gibeah, none of the residents would take him into their home.[35] This was a blatant disregard of Israelite hospitality practices. Finally, an old man from the Levite's hometown graciously offered to host him, as he was living in Gibeah and did not want him to sleep in the open square. The Levite offered to provide for his own food, even though the custom said the host should feed him and his companions. Once they were settled in, the house was surrounded by men described as worthless.[36] They demanded that the old man turn over the Levite, so they could 'know' him. (This is the same play on words used by the men of Sodom).

Similar to the Genesis account, these men wanted to rape the Levite guest. This is clearly evident by the statements made by the old man:

- Do not commit this outrage. (Judges 19:23)
- Take my virgin daughter and my concubine and *humble* them. (The Hebrew word for humble is *anah*. It means to afflict, oppress or abuse. (Judges 19:24)
- He told the men of Gibeah to do with the women 'whatever you want'. (Judges 19:24)

It is so blatantly clear that this passage does not refer to homosexuality. They wanted to 'humble' this visitor. In the Genesis passage, women were offered to the men for their thirst for oppression and abuse. Unlike the men of Sodom, these Israelites, in the Judges passage, took the Levite's concubine and raped her all night long. They abused her to the point that she died on the old man's doorstep the next morning. Their 'encounter' with the concubine was not about sex. It was about control, abuse and domination. This is not how people engage in legitimate sexual behavior. Judges 20 talks about the penalty the tribe of Benjamin had to pay, once they were confronted, for not only committing this crime, but their attempt to cover it up. The fact that the Levite gave his concubine to the men is further proof that this passage was not about homosexuality. Why did he not give them his male servant if the gang was comprised of wanton homosexual men? A male servant or slave was the lowest on the social scale. In the Genesis passage, Lot's daughters were the lowest on this scale in Lot's home, so they were offered. In the Judges passage, this male slave was the lowest, yet he was not offered. Why not? Because the old man understood the intent of the men of Gibeah was to humiliate the visitor, not engage in homosexual sex. By having sex with the Levite's concubine, the Levite experienced a level of humiliation as she was 'married' to him, where the slave was not as close to him. Raping the slave would not have fulfilled their purposes.

When opponents of homosexuality quote scriptures, they do not mention this passage. Dr. Richard Mouw is the president of Fuller Theological Seminary in Pasadena, California. He has served at Fuller for approximately 20 years, being the institution's president since 1993. Dr. Mouw stated in an interview for the documentary, *For The Bible Tells Me So*, that he believes the story of Sodom and Gomorrah is about homosexuality and not hospitality.

> "If all we have is the Sodom and Gomorrah story, there is not a lot in the Old Testament that settles the question [about the validity or sinfulness of homosexuality]. We have to turn to the New Testament."[37]

Here is another example of a well-intentioned, but ill informed Bible scholar discussing the issue of homosexuality. How is the President of one of the nations' leading evangelical seminaries unaware of this passage in Judges 19? If he was aware of this account at the time of his interview, how could he make the statement that there is 'not a lot in the Old Testament'? Most disconcerting, Dr. Mouw is also a professor with three earned graduate degrees, according to the Fuller Theological Seminary website. Maybe it is a misunderstanding of the text on his part, so he didn't mention it. This quote was from a documentary that I did not personally edit, so I will give Dr. Mouw the benefit of doubt. Maybe his mention of the Judges passage is "on the cutting room floor". However, I doubt it. I do not know Dr. Mouw but his statement about homosexuality, again, sounds like the preconceived and unsubstantiated rhetoric that is being taught in many Christian churches and seminaries. The text clearly references *inhospitable acts* especially when compared to the eighteenth chapter of Genesis, the words of the prophet Ezekiel[38] and the words of Jesus Christ. I guess Dr. Mouw did not see the connection. Sadly, his statement contributes to the abundance of incorrect teaching about homosexuality. The Judges passage not only confirms the inhospitable acts in ancient Israel, but it also invalidates the accusation that the crime of Sodom was homosexuality. Since there is no way for any scholar to justify the Israelites' actions or misinterpret the meaning found in Judges 19, the passage seems to be simply ignored.

Leviticus 20:13

"If a man lies with a man as one lies with a woman, both of them have done what is detestable. They must be put to death; their blood will be on their own heads."

Upon reading this passage, certain people will say "See, it's in the Bible. Homosexuality is wrong." This is just one verse that resides within the Old Testament law that was specifically given to ancient Israel. There are 31,101 other verses in the Bible. This one verse cannot be the sole basis for an entire doctrine or teaching. It is not good hermeneutical practice. Scriptures need to always be interpreted properly and to the best of one's ability. A cursory 'reading' of scripture coupled with a definitive and incorrect interpretation, is what turns people away from wanting to learn about the God of the Bible. God had good and purposeful intentions when He instituted this command for the Israelite men. This command means what it says. Two men are not to have sexual intercourse as a man and a woman do. The command was not given based on the described behavior, but the outcome of the behavior. Therefore, we need to try to determine the purpose behind this verse, how it applies to the remainder of scripture, if at all and most importantly, Christians today.

In Genesis 1:28 God instructed the man and woman to conceive and bear many children and fill up the earth. This was not an exclusive command to Adam and Eve, but a general command for all of mankind at the time. God created an entire world and wanted it full of people who would worship Him. Sexual activity between two males would not fulfill the command to be fruitful and multiply. Does this mean that homosexual orientation is sinful? You cannot arrive at this conclusion simply from this verse. We do know that God did not want men to have sexual intercourse with each other; however we are not given a reason why, other than to keep the Israelites behavior distinct from the Egyptians and the Canaanites.[39] We can draw an inference from the Genesis 1 command that same gender sexual activity would be a violation. The Leviticus passage says for a man to lie with a man is a *tow`ebah*, the Hebrew word translated into the English word *abomination*. Some Bible translations use the word *detestable*. This is an incorrect translation as detestable is a derivative of the English word, *abomination*, not the Hebrew word, *tow`ebah*. In English, abomination has a stronger connotation than *tow`ebah*. In English, abomination means to utterly detest, loathe or be disgusted by something. However, the contextual meaning of the Hebrew word *tow`ebah* is closer to violation, forbidden or unclean. The Hebrew word for abomination means illegal and is used to describe a wide range of 'wrongs'. Here are some sins that are an abomination: idolatry (Deuteronomy 7:25, Deuteronomy 13), cheating (Deuteronomy 25:13-19, Proverbs 11:1), and dishonesty (Proverbs 12:22). Proverbs 6:16 says the following are abominable: *a proud look, a lying tongue, shedding innocent blood and devising wicked plans.* With the exception of killing someone, most of us have been guilty of one of these sins at some point. Due to this variety, the definition of abomination cannot be as severe as it is commonly taught. This word has been given its 'detestable' definition by modern society based upon its feelings towards homosexuality. Proverbs 3:32 gives a better context of abomination. "For the froward person is an abomination to the Lord." A froward person is one with a twisted heart. He breaks rules. Basically, he engages in improper behavior.

So, the man who lies with another man is one who has broken the rules. Furthermore, the scriptures state that he is to be put to death, just like the adulterer, those who curse their parents and those who work on the Sabbath – in the Christian tradition, Sunday. [40] This is a pretty strong penalty for these behaviors. It is interesting to note that Christians and non-Christians alike, state that homosexuals are to be put to death, but they do not quote the verse that says adulterers are to be put to death. There are no picket signs being carried proclaiming that liars and the prideful are an abomination to God. There is a lack of protest because no one really cares.

A passage in the book of Leviticus instructs men **and women** not to have sex with animals, but it only instructs **men** to not have sex with each other. <u>Why were women left out of the prohibition of homosexuality?</u> There has to be significance in the latter prohibition for men, as God is not forgetful and 'skipped' over female homosexuality. As stated before, God was building a nation of people, so procreation was paramount. A man's seed was viewed as the sole element that brought forth life. Women are only spoken of as the bearer of the children. Her biological contribution is not referenced; just her performance in childbirth. As you read through the Old Testament, the word seed (*Zehrah* in Hebrew) is referred to as an offspring, child or man's semen. When Abel was killed in Genesis 4, God appointed another seed (child). God promised to multiply Abraham's seed exceedingly.[41] A man's seed was critical to the building of the Hebrew nation and could not be wasted. Hence, men were not allowed to have sex with each other, so precious seed would not be wasted. This is why Genesis 38:9 records Onan being punished for spilling his seed on the ground. He was not masturbating, as many Christian traditions teach. He did not want to impregnate his dead brother's wife. This is not an issue in modern society. The laws found in Leviticus and Deuteronomy are also known as purity laws. They were essential in keeping the nation of Israel separate and distinguishable from other nations and people. These laws were not *moral* laws.

In contemporary times, neither adultery nor homosexuality is punishable by death. The Old Testament penalties for breaking these laws do not have a current application. In the chapter on Old Testament Law and New Testament Grace, I mentioned that modern day Christians are not obligated to keep the Old Testament Law unless it has been reinstated by Jesus in the New Testament. Leviticus 20:13 is a part of that same law. It is housed with other commands that are not observed in today's culture and society. Here are a few:

> Lev 19:9-10 instructed the Israelites when gleaning their vineyards, to leave the grapes that are in the corners of the vineyards for the poor. This is a good principle to remember the poor and to provide for them when we can, but it is not a direct command to be kept.

> Lev 19:19 gives instructions to not cross pollinate seeds and not to wear clothing that has mixed fabrics (i.e. Wool-blends, cotton-blends, etc.)

> Lev 19:28 instructed the Israelites to have no tattoos. Acquiring tattoos is widely practiced in our society, by Jewish and Christian people as well as the non-religious.

Like previously mentioned, Jesus came to fulfill the Old Testament law. If modern day Christians are obligated to keep any of it, we are required to keep all of it, which is not possible. Leviticus 20:13 is a part of this law. The scripture that instructs men to not sleep with each other (along with the other scriptural mandates that are not observed today), served a specific purpose for ancient Israel. Those laws and restrictions are irrelevant today. The prohibition of male homosexuality referenced in the Leviticus and Deuteronomy scriptures are most likely related to the pagan practices of other Near East cultures mentioned on page 73. Thus, a prohibition of homosexuality cannot be based on these verses alone.

Bestiality

The practice of men or women having sex with animals is often brought up in the same conversation about homosexuality. Homosexuality is said to be a sin just like bestiality is a sin. Not only does bestiality have nothing to do with homosexuality, the description of its nature and punishment is far more severe than that of homosexual behavior in the Old Testament law.

In Leviticus 18:22-23, a man lying with a man is an abomination – a broken rule or improper behavior. However, a person who lies with an animal, not only defiles themselves but it is defined as a perversion. When a person was defiled in the Old Testament, they were rendered ceremoniously unclean. This was not a permanent state. A woman was considered unclean during her menstrual cycle and it was an abomination to have sex with her during this time.[42] Defilement was not the main issue with bestiality. The Hebrew word for perversion is *tebel*. It means confusion, or against the natural order of things. If homosexual activity is unnatural (as categorized by the religious and non-religious), why was it not labeled as *tebel*? This verse would be the logical place to make that statement. Homosexuality does not go against the natural order of things. It is just not common as heterosexuality. Homosexuality does not produce offspring. It is an unnatural practice for those who are exclusively heterosexual; however homosexual orientation does not exist in exclusively heterosexual people. Some homosexual people feel that heterosexuality is just as unnatural for them. Many people fit within the wide spectrum between exclusive homosexuality and exclusive heterosexuality. Most people are right-handed. This does not mean that left-handed people are confused and go against the nature of things. They are just different. However, history shows left-handed people were not always treated with respect and acceptance.

In summary, the Old Testament clearly does not give a general condemnation of homosexuality. The books of Genesis and Judges show how a specific sexual behavior was being used to humiliate and socially degrade men. Women were not excluded from this form of degradation. Leviticus is not an eternal pronouncement against homosexuality, just like its prohibition on tattoos is not relevant for contemporary times. Furthermore, Leviticus cannot be a general condemnation of homosexuality, as lesbianism is not mentioned. This book addresses a behavior and a custom that God did not want His people, ancient Israel, to engage in, namely male homosexual acts which were used to degrade and humiliate. The Levitical regulation is about distinguishing God's people from other nations, not condemning homosexuality, in general.

CHAPTER 8
My First Kiss

The summer of 1985 seemed so amorous. The days were bright. The sun was warm. People scurried around like rabbits. Ladies hit the mall for new outfits. Guys washed, waxed and detailed their cars on an almost daily basis. It was the summer and it was about the look…the lookers and the looked at. Six years later, Will Smith's song, "Summertime", would describe it precisely. I drove a 1970 Gold Chevy Nova. One of my female friends named it the "G-Ride". When you are 19 years old, life seems invincible. I would cruise the G-Ride anywhere and sadly in any operating condition as long as it was clean. I remember driving one Saturday when I knew my brakes were bad. OK, bad is an understatement! They were shot to the curb. They were, basically, inoperable. My buddy John and I were driving north on Sepulveda Blvd. through Culver City and I needed to pull over at a gas station to put some water in my radiator. I saw a gas station, changed lanes and pressed the brake pedal to slow down. My car started laughing at me as my speed did not decrease. It felt like it sped up. John yelled at me, "Slow down man". "I caaaan't", I returned as both of my feet were now on the pedal. I quickly pumped the brakes again, hit a dip, and the car bounced up and slowed to a thud in front of the gas pump! "Man, you don't have any brakes! I'm never ridin' wit' you again." John screamed. He wasn't a Los Angeles native. He was from the "islands". He was a little reserved, but he was my buddy. "How are you gonna get home? You gotta ride with me." I responded. I knew the temporary remedy for my inability to stop. I needed brake fluid. I popped the hood, told John to fill the radiator while I went inside for brake fluid. Our trip to the mall to check out girls was short circuited. John topped off the radiator and I topped off the master cylinder and we flipped a U-turn and headed back to LA in search of my brother, the mechanic.

Later that day, I found myself at Trak Auto buying brake pads and 'beauty supplies' for the G-Ride. My brother had bled my brakes earlier, after giving me the big brother lecture on driving without brakes. He had a lot of nerve. He would drive his car without tires if he could get away with it. As I was walking down the aisle looking for Armour-All for my tires, this guy caught my eye. I don't know what it was, but he had my attention. He looked up at me and nodded his head. I nodded back with a slight smile and continued my search. I found the Armour-All and moved to a different aisle. I was walking with my head down, again searching. I looked up and the guy I had my eye on was right in front of me. This time he smiled and kind of chuckled. I guess it was safe for him to smile because I almost ran into him. "Wassup?" I asked. He said, "Hi." Now, I had a closer look at him. He was handsome. Actually he was beautiful, in a masculine way. My heart started to beat faster and I wondered what was happening. I had admired guys before, but never like this and definitely not this close. But it was more than that. I saw something in him. The boy definitely was not from LA. He was desperately in need of a haircut and wasn't wearing a hat. LA boys don't come outside without covering up their 'tore-up' heads. His mini-fro didn't distract me though. As we continued to shop, we kept noticing each other and would exchange a polite smile. 'Is he trying to get my attention?' I thought. Eventually, he made his purchase and left the store. I got in line, finished my transaction and headed for the door. As soon as the sunshine hit my face, I heard his voice again.

"Do you know where I can get a good haircut around here?" Now that was the question he should have been asking.

"Uh, uh, uh, yeah, um, I'm not sure. Uh, my barber is far from here. I mean you would have to drive. Are you from LA?" I managed to get all of that out without looking too stupid. His full lips parted, revealing a beautiful set of teeth as he was smiling again.

"No, I'm visiting my sister and her boyfriend for the summer. I wanted to drive around town so I came to get some oil for her car. I'm Terrell."

He extended his hand and I shook it.

"Oh, well I'm sure there is a barber somewhere around here. Probably in the shopping center across the street."

I had no idea where a barber shop was but I was caught off guard by him.

"Do you think you could show me?"

I pointed. He just stood there. I asked him,

"Did you wait for me to come out of the store just to ask me for a barber?"

"Yes...and no. I don't know anybody here and you seemed cool, so I thought I'd wait for you."

This guy was flirting with me. What the heck? I never had a guy flirt with me before, so I wasn't 100% sure. It certainly seemed like it. Actually I was hoping he was because I would have never gotten the nerve to flirt with him. All I could say back was, "Oh, I see." Terrell put his bag in his sister's car and I dropped my stuff in my brother's car. He would let me borrow it every now and then. I walked with Terrell across the street to the other shopping center. He told me where he was from, why he came to LA, and that he was undecided about college as he had just graduated the month before. I graduated the year before. As we approached the barber shop, he stopped walking, turned to me and said,

"You are really cute. Is there anywhere we can go dancing?"
I almost fell down. I looked around to see if anyone else heard what he just said.

"Dancing? Like you and me dancing? No, I don't know any place to go dancing?"

There was no way in the world I was going to be seen dancing with a guy in public. Where could two guys go to dance? Thoughts were whirling around in my head. Boy, did I have a lot to learn. He could see I was a little uncomfortable.

"Well, maybe we can do something else. Are you free later?"

"Uh, yeah, I guess so.", I answered in a daze.

"Let me give you my sister's number. Hopefully we can go do something later."

"Yeah, Okay, cool."

"Thanks, Kev. I'll see you later."

He disappeared into the barber shop. Then I panicked. Who saw me talking to this guy? My cousin owned a store about 5 doors down from the barber shop. I wondered if he saw me talking with this guy. I walked the opposite way of my cousin's store and found my way back to my brother's car and drove home to fix the G-Ride.

~~ O ~~

I was shaking all over when I dialed the number Terrell gave me. I didn't know what to say. I looked down the hall to see where my mother was and then closed my bedroom door. A man with a real husky voice answered the phone, "Hello?"

"Hi, can I speak with Terrell?"

"Yeah, hold on."

"Hello?" It was Terrell.

"Hi Terrell. It's Kevin from earlier today."

"Hey man, I was hoping you would call. What are you doing?"

"If you want to go hang out, we could go to the beach or something."

"That's real cool. Can you pick me up? I can't take my sister's car."

"At your sister's house? Her boyfriend will be there? That's kinda weird."

"Oh. He's real cool. I'm out to my sister. He knows I'm gay too."

Gay? He's gay? Am I gay? My thoughts were bouncing off the ceiling. I never gave it a label. My attraction to guys, that is. I mostly ignored it. Terrell gave me the address to his sister's condo and an hour later I was ringing the doorbell. I stood nervously on the porch waiting....waiting...and waiting. Finally, a tall huge brown skinned brotha answered the door. I was scared out of my mind. I had never done anything like this before. I actually was picking up a guy for...a date.

"Hey man, you must be here for Terrell. I'm Will. Come on in and have a seat."

"I'm Kevin. Thanks." This guy was all man. He didn't have that macho BS thing going. He was just very masculine. He appeared to be just as strong on the inside as he was on the outside. He was about 35 years old. He yelled upstairs to Terrell,

"Terrell, your date is here."

Then he turned to me, "Kevin, right? Would you like a beer or something?"

Date? A beer? Wow. Not only was Will a cool brotha, he was treating me like a man. I guess I expected something less. This was 1985.

"Naw thanks. I'm cool."

I didn't want to appear to be a punk, but I didn't drink. Plus, I was underage, but Will hadn't carded me so I guess he didn't care. Will engaged me in small talk while I waited for Terrell.

"So what are you young guys gettin' into tonight?"

"Probably head down to the beach or something."

"Cool."

Finally, Terrell came down. Boy did he look good with his fresh hightop fade haircut.

"I'm leaving your phone number with Will. We just met so I wanna be safe." He said.

"No problem."

"I wrote down your license number too."

Will started to laugh.

"Terrell, the man doesn't look like a serial killer to me. You guys have fun."

I let out a nervous laugh. Then, Terrell and I took off. I drove Terrell around LA and eventually down to the beach. We walked and talked for a couple of hours and got to know one another. He had never been to the beach. He was in awe at the enormity of the ocean. He mentioned he was going to find a job, so he wouldn't be broke during the summer. On the drive back to his place, he said he was going to find a gay club where we could go dancing. For a young guy, he was pretty aware of 'gay culture'. He looked older than eighteen, so back home he could get into clubs and bars. He figured he'd be able to do the same thing here. I pulled in front of his sister's townhouse and he thanked me for taking him out. Then he smiled and just stared at me. I began to be uncomfortable.

"What?" I asked him.

"You've never kissed a guy, huh?"

He went straight for the jugular. I hadn't kissed a guy and did not expect to. I guess I wanted to, but kissing guys wasn't something you did in my neighborhood. Gay guys were talked about like dogs. They were all 'swishy' and scary. They couldn't defend themselves. They talked with high pitched voices and whined. That was the stereotype anyway.

"No, uh, I've never kissed a guy before."

"Have you kissed a girl?" he asked.

"Of course."

It wasn't like I had kissed a lot of girls, but I did have some experience in that department.

"Well, kissing is kissing. Except with a guy, its better. Wanna see?"

Before I knew what was coming out of my mouth, I said, "Yea..." Terrell leaned over to me and gave me this long and soft peck on my lips. The only description for what I felt was 'electric'. I don't know if it was his moustache or shock of the first time, but it was the best feeling I had ever had. It was pretty unbelievable. I definitely didn't expect that. I didn't want him to stop, but he did.

"Are you OK?" he whispered.

"Yeah, I'm great...now."

He leaned over and kissed me again. This time I kissed him back. It just felt right. It felt natural. In the middle of kissing him, I started to miss it.

I knew we would have to stop at some point, but I wanted it to last forever. We kissed for a while, and then Terrell said he had to go. We said goodnight and from the car, I watched him walk inside. I drove away buzzed. I had kissed a guy and it was incredible. I don't know how I got home, but I did.

I couldn't wait for Terrell to call me again, but he never did. I had lost his number, so I waited for him. The phone never rang. Weeks later, I found his number. I dialed it and Will answered. He told me Terrell went back home a few days after we met. His mother got sick and he wanted to be with her. I understood and hung up the phone. I was glad to have met Terrell and appreciative of his gift to me...my first kiss.

CHAPTER 9
Marriage & Adultery

There is a colloquialism used within Christian church culture to describe a wife. It is 'help meet'. This is how the Hebrew word *Ezer* is translated in the original King James version of the Bible. In the following quote, the New King James version translates Genesis 2:20 to say 'there was no *helper comparable* to him.'

Genesis 2:18-23

And the LORD God said, "*It is* not good that man should be alone; I will make him a helper comparable to him." Out of the ground the LORD God formed every beast of the field and every bird of the air, and brought *them* to Adam to see what he would call them. And whatever Adam called each living creature that *was* its name. So Adam gave names to all cattle, to the birds of the air, and to every beast of the field. But for Adam there was not found a helper comparable to him. And the LORD God caused a deep sleep to fall on Adam, and he slept; and He took one of his ribs, and closed up the flesh in its place. Then the rib which the LORD God had taken from man He made into a woman, and He brought her to the man. And Adam said:
"This *is* now bone of my bones
And flesh of my flesh;
She shall be called Woman,
Because she was taken out of Man."

This verse is referencing a companion for Adam. The word Ezer simply means help, helper, relief or assistance. The word by itself has no connotation of being suitable or comparable. However, the context of the passage infers suitability or comparability based on what happened to Adam in verse 18 and 19, as well as Adam's response in verse 23 after Eve was created. Verse 18 says that God will bring Adam 'help' or 'someone who helps'. In verse 19, God creates all of the animals and in verse 20, Adam names them. God then says 'no help was found for Adam.' In essence, God brought all of these beings before Adam for help but none of them were comparable to him. The animals were obviously a help to Adam, as animals assist us today. However, they were not human, so they were not a comparable help. They could not help Adam fulfill his complete calling to fill and subdue the earth. Subdue gives the connotation of the earth being wild and untamed. Subdue means to force under subjection. The animals played a part in this role but they were not sufficient enough to fulfill it. Eve was a comparable helper to him because she was human like Adam versus the animals that were presented in verses 19-20.

When Genesis says it was not good for Adam to be alone, it was not referring to loneliness. Adam needed someone of his kind. It was not sufficient for him to be the only one of his kind in the earth. In verse 23 Adam acknowledges that Eve was one of his kind. Verse 23 can best be translated from Hebrew to say, "*This time here is someone that is of my essence and substance, with a body like mine...*" Verse 24 continues with what has traditionally been defined as the first mention of marriage. There is a hermeneutical law called "Law of First Mention". When reading Genesis 2:24, we must determine what is being *mentioned* and discover if anything else is being mentioned. Is the subject of marriage, the creation of a family, both or neither being mentioned in the verse? The creation of children is mentioned because the phrase 'one flesh' means to become one family, not one spiritual or symbolic body. Only a heterosexual union can produce children, so this verse is the *first mention* of the 'future' occurrence of childbirth. The verse establishes a pattern for conception. However, conception may not be the only subject mentioned because the phrase 'one flesh' also means one clan, which also defines the many extended families of the Old Testament. Additionally, Old Testament marriage does not have one type of representation. Although there were some monogamous marriages, many marriages were polygamous, as well as Levirate marriages, where a man married his dead brother's wife, so she could provide an heir for her deceased husband. If verse 24 is indeed describing marriage, did it describe all types of marriage in the Old Testament? Does it describe marriage as we know it today? The answer to both questions is no.

In order to answer this question, we need to understand the meaning and origin of marriage. Our traditional and contemporary idea of marriage is not an original concept in Old Testament Hebrew or New Testament Greek. The first instances of the word marry or marriage, in the Old Testament, has to do with Levirate marriage duties, conjugal rights and praise.[43] None of these passages give an example of what we know marriage to be today.

The English word marriage originated around 1297 A.D. Its etymology comes from the Old French word *marier* and from the Latin word, *maritare*. Etymologically, it means to wed, marry or give in marriage. Contemporary marriage can be defined as *a social institution whereby a legal or religious ceremony formalizes the decision, a man and woman have already made, to live as husband and wife, including the accompanying social festivities.* [Emphasis mine] The key to the definition of marriage is that a man and a woman first *decide* to live as husband and wife, and then their union is formalized legally and/or religiously. Genesis 2:2 is the first mention of a *union* between a man and a woman.

In Christian tradition, biblical marriage is an institution defined by the concept of a 'one flesh' union. The original King James version of Genesis 2:24 reads,

> "Therefore shall a man leave his father and his mother, and shall *cleave* unto his wife: and they shall be *one flesh*." [Italics mine]

These two people will become one flesh and the *man* shall cleave unto his wife. This concept of 'one flesh' cannot be separated from 'cleaving' as it is all one process. In Hebrew, the word *cleave* means to stick together like glue, to cling, to stay close. The term *one flesh* means one body, flesh or kindred. The overall idea of Genesis 2:24 is that a man will leave his original household or family and stick to a new family that he creates. He will cling to his new woman / wife. They will be so close as to be one body or one body of people – one kindred, one family[44]. Traditional teaching says that 'one flesh' indicates the sexual union in a marriage. The Hebrew term *Basar* would have to be used metaphorically to mean one flesh, since two individuals really cannot become one body. The entrance of a man's penis into a woman's vagina does not transform them into one body. When he withdraws, they do not become two bodies again. What many Christians believe is that 'one flesh' is a spiritual concept. God created Adam from the dust of the ground. Eve was created from the substance of Adam's body. Since the raw materials for Eve's creation existed in Adam's body, they are considered to be 'one flesh'. However, the context of the verse is the creation of a family. The man leaves his parents and family and creates a new one (one flesh or kindred). This command was given to Adam. The command could not mean something different to us today than it originally meant for Adam. Adam did not have an earthly mother and father like we do today. God was his only parent. So what did God mean for Adam when He said to leave your 'mother and father'? The Hebrew words *ab* and *em* are translated mother and father, respectively. Ab can be defined as 'a father of an individual'. However, it also means God as a father, an originator, a producer or a generator. This makes sense as God *created* Adam. The word *em* means mother of humans. Adam did not have a mother in the natural sense. The command to leave mother and father was not just given to future mankind. It was explicitly given to Adam, so how would Adam have understood the concept of a mother prior to Eve giving birth? The word *em* (mother) also means 'point of departure or division'. We understand that in childbirth, a mother is a point of departure. However, in Adam's case, his point of departure was God Himself. He was to depart from his family, which was made up of God and himself, in order to create his own family. This is a clearer understanding of 'one flesh'. One flesh is not so much about the joining of the man and the woman as it is about the new family unit they will create. This understanding of 'one flesh' lines up with God's command in Genesis 1:28 when He said to 'be fruitful, multiply and fill the earth'. His command was not 'get married' or 'take a wife'. The command was to build families in the earth.

Traditional biblical thought says that this 'first' marriage between Adam and Eve established the basis of contemporary marriage, which is *only* between one man and one woman. As we take a closer look at Old Testament scripture, we will be able to determine if Genesis 2:24 was truly the established pattern for marriage, if everyone followed the pattern and if marriage was a requirement for all relationships?

Old Testament Marriage

> "The central ritual of the marriage ceremony itself was the symbolic bringing of the bride into the groom's house, followed by great rejoicing. Song of Solomon 3:11 describes the bridegroom as wearing a special crown given to him by his mother, and in Isaiah 61:10 he wears a garland. A later description relates that the bride was escorted to meet the groom, and the groom came out with his friends accompanied by musicians and the sound of tambourines (1 Maccabees 9:37-39). The bride wore her finest clothes, many jewels (Isaiah 61:10), and a veil (Genesis 29:23-25; Song of Solomon 4:1). There followed a lengthy celebration with merrymaking, singing (Jeremiah 16:9), and feasting often lasting a week or two (Judges 14:12)."[45]

In western culture, when we hear of someone getting 'married', we envision a wedding ceremony, a reception, gifts, and a honeymoon. This tradition has been passed down from ancient celebrations. Some ancient marriages were arranged, as we find in the case with Jacob and Rachel.[46] This type of arranged marriage would have included a celebration. The arrangement for this marriage was made between Jacob and Laban, Rachel's father. Even though Laban did not honor his end of the arrangement, nonetheless, an arrangement of marriage was made. In other cases, men acquired wives, as Boaz did with Ruth. He had much respect and desire for her. She was an employee and worked on his property. He treated her very well. He had purchased some land and 'acquired' Ruth along with the property. Ruth became his wife. Ruth was not a random acquisition; Boaz wanted her and followed this property acquisition custom to get her. These are two examples of one man choosing and marrying one wife, just as Adam took Eve to be his wife.

Multiple Wives

In Genesis 4:19, we read about a different type of marriage. Lamech took for himself, *two* wives. This is a different pattern from what we read in Genesis 2. This is the first record in scripture of a man taking more than one wife. Lamech was only six generations from Adam. After the Great Flood, Abram (later renamed Abraham) was married to Sarai (later renamed Sarah). Sarai was unable to conceive so she gave Abram her female servant, Hagar. Genesis 16:3 tells us that Hagar became Abram's *wife* and bore him a son. There is no indication that God disapproved of this additional relationship. This was not adultery. Thirteen years later, God blesses Abraham with a son through his first wife, Sarah and establishes His covenant with him. The practice of men having multiple wives continues throughout the Old Testament. Jacob, Abraham's grandson, had twelve sons for whom the 12 tribes of Israel were named. Jacob was married to two women who were sisters, Leah and Rachel. The mothers of Jacob's children were his two wives and his two concubines. Abraham and Jacob are two examples of marriages that do not fit into the 'model' of the Genesis 2:24 verse where it is assumed that its definition of marriage is to be between *one* man and *one* woman only. There is no record of God condemning either of these relationships.

We read that hundreds of years later, Jesus is asked about divorce. Jesus quoted Genesis 2:24 and stated that Moses allowed for divorce because of the hardness of men's hearts, then said, "but from the beginning it was not so." What could Jesus have been referring to, when He said, 'but from the beginning it was not so'? He could not have been referring to marriage being between only one man and one woman because Moses was not even born at the time of Abraham and Jacob's multiple 'marriages'. In Matthew 19, Jesus also stated that if a man 'put his wife away' and married another wife, he was committing adultery. If adultery is breaking the 'model' of Genesis 2:24, were not Abraham and Jacob already adulterers? There is no condemnation from God stating Abraham and Jacob were adulterers. Why? Adultery is about the breaking of commitment more than additional sexual and/or marital unions.

Abraham and Jacob remained committed to their wives and concubines. They cared for them and all of these women remained in their respective households. Jacob was so committed to Rachel that he worked an additional seven years to get her, after his father-in-law reneged on their original agreement.

Additional wives held a different status in their households. A hierarchy existed. The first or main wife was revered first. Additional wives followed and concubines came after them. The purpose of additional wives and concubines was to bear more children and provide for the man's sexual pleasure. However, the entire group was viewed as one family. The Bible uses a Hebrew word that means 'household' or 'clan'. It is the same word for 'one flesh'.

Matthew 19:7-8

They said to Jesus, "Why then did Moses command to give a certificate of divorce, and to put her away?"
Jesus said to them, "Moses, because of the hardness of your hearts, permitted you to *divorce* your wives, but from the beginning it was not so.

In Matthew 19:7, Jesus was asked about two conjoined but distinct events that are often read as one event. He was asked why Moses required the man to give his wife a <u>bill of divorce</u> and then for his wife to <u>be put away</u>. A bill of divorce was a document given from a man to a woman releasing her from the marriage. Moses instituted this procedure because men were putting away their wives for any reason. The phrase, 'put her away' means to dismiss from the family, to set loose, to detain no longer. This means that

<u>divorces</u> were not given before Moses' command. Wives were simply commanded to leave. In ancient Israel, a woman's survival depended upon the man to whom she was married. If she was simply let go or dismissed, she would have to return to her father's house, if possible, or live in destitution, as no other man would want to marry her. The bill of divorce would increase her chances of remarrying. When the passage in Matthew is normally read, it is read from a perspective of 'what makes a divorce biblically approved or authorized?' In other words, what do I need to do to get around the restriction on divorcing? Traditional interpretation of the biblical text suggests that a person cannot get divorced if sexual immorality is not involved. It is interesting to note how Jesus viewed the issue. When He was asked about divorcing and then the dismissing of wives, He didn't address the divorcing part of the question. He addressed the dismissing part. Scholars have changed the modern translations to read 'permitted you to *divorce* your wives.' This is not correct. The correct translation is 'permitted you to *put your wives away*.' The Greek words used in verse 8 are *apoluo autos* (put away), not *apostasion* (divorce). Jesus went on to say, "Therefore what God has joined together, let not man separate." [47] He was more concerned with the commitment that was being broken than the legal aspects of divorce. Jesus was saying 'because you were hardheaded, Moses let you break your commitment and send your wives away.' What was 'not so in the beginning' was wives were not put away. In the Old Testament, if and when a man acquired a new wife, the previous wife remained. This is evidenced by King David's multiple wives. Men remained committed to their spouses, at least

on a level of providing for them and allowing them to remain in the family. Jesus took this opportunity to clarify His position on remaining committed to your spouse.

Adultery and Fidelity

If marital faithfulness to one wife was critical in Israel's history, why were there Levitical laws in existence, instructing men on how to treat additional wives and concubines? After King David impregnated Bathsheba and killed her husband, God spoke through the prophet Nathan and told David that He (God) gave to David, Saul's wives and would have given him more![48] How could adultery be defined as having a relationship with more than one woman, if God *authorized* it for David? Deuteronomy 21:10-17 gives instructions on how a man can take a woman captive from his enemy when the '*Lord your God delivers him into [your] hands'* and make her your wife. The scripture goes on to regulate how she must be treated fairly. Then it gives instructions on how inheritance is split between the sons from two different *wives!* This command also invalidates the prohibition of adultery, if marriage is indeed defined as one husband and one wife. Could it be that the Christian church's traditional understanding of adultery is not correct? Maybe we need to correctly define it.

In a different type of example, Genesis 39 tells the story of a man named Potiphar, whose wife was attracted to Joseph, the overseer of Potiphar's house. Potiphar's wife wanted to have sex with Joseph but he refused and told her,

> "There is no one greater in this house than I, nor
> has he [Potiphar] kept back anything from me but
> you, because you are his wife. How then can I do
> this great wickedness, and sin against God?" [49]

Joseph was committed to God. Why did he believe that he would be
committing a sin against God by sleeping with Potiphar's wife? We
just read that King David and other men had multiple wives. If
Joseph had sex with her, would it really be illicit and unlawful? The
answer is yes. Joseph made no commitment to her. Potiphar and
his wife were in a committed relationship, thus Potiphar had the
right to have sex with her and she with him. She was not in a
committed relationship with Joseph, so for him to sleep with her
would be a sin. Adultery was the sin of breaking covenant with the
one to whom you were **committed**. If Joseph slept with Potiphar's
wife, she would have been an adulteress. By sleeping with her, he
would have become an adulterer. The issue at hand was not sex, but
commitment.

During ancient times, marriage was a man-driven institution.
Men married women and took care of them. Socially and
economically, women depended on men. Men had no real
dependence upon women. Sadly, women were dispensable. There
was always another wife or concubine to have sex with or to take
care of and bear the children. This is why Moses required a bill of
divorce, to protect the 'rights' of women. Moses was the first
women's rights advocate! Based on these relationship examples (and
the many relationships that followed them), there is no scriptural
support to say that marriage is only between one man and one

woman. It was clearly up to the man's discretion. Therefore, the traditional definition of marriage *cannot* be based upon Genesis 2:24. Why? Contemporary marriage, traditionally and legally, is not a biblical construct. It is a social construct. Socially, the definition of marriage has been 'the state of being united to a person of the opposite sex as husband and wife in a consensual and contractual relationship as recognized by law.' Society developed this law based on a faulty understanding of scripture. This definition of marriage is quite different from the biblical practice we read about. So it begs the question. If a man is able to choose the number of wives he may have, what prevents him from choosing the gender of his spouse? In the coming section on New Testament marriage, we will see how the institution of marriage has changed over the years and the different views and opinions the ancient church fathers held about marriage and marital relationships.

Concubines

A concubine was a female slave who functioned as a secondary wife and surrogate mother.[50] Oftentimes, a man's concubine was also his wife's maidservant. The usage of the term, concubine, generally "signifies an ongoing, quasi-matrimonial relationship where the woman is of lower social status than the man with whom she is conjugal and/or his official wife or wives."[51] When the word concubine is translated in the Old Testament, it is from one of two Hebrew words: Piylegesh or Ishshah. The word Piylegesh has a connotation of softness or pleasure.[52] The main purpose of Piylegesh was for sexual companionship. The Hebrew word Ishshah means wife or woman. In some context, a reference to a concubine was no different than that of a man's wife; in other context, she was his sexual servant. Genesis 35:22 lists Bilhah as Jacob's concubine (Piylegesh). Her purpose was just for pleasure. This may be why Jacob's son Reuben felt that he could also have sex with her.[53]

Judges 19 is the story about a Levite man and his concubine (Ishshah). Notice that the Hebrew word for the Levite's concubine is Ishshah, the same word for wife. Some Bible scholars do not understand the relationship between adultery, wives and concubines.

> "The Levite's concubine was recognized as one of his wives, but she did not have the same status in the home or in society as his primary wife had. In this sense, a concubine was an authorized mistress. Many prominent men in the Old Testament had concubines. Examples include Abraham (Genesis 25:6), Jacob (Genesis 35:22), Caleb (1 Chronicles 2:46), Saul (2 Samuel 3:7), David (2 Samuel 5:13), Solomon (1 Kings 11:3 — 300 concubines), and Rehoboam (2 Chronicles 11:21). Significantly, we never see this kind of family life blessed by God."[54]

It is interesting that this Bible commentator says that God did not bless the family life of men with concubines. There is no biblical support for this position. Actually, Abraham and Solomon are stark contradictions to this statement. This commentator is not the only one with this opinion. Pastor Chuck Smith said the following about the Levite in Judges 19,

> "Now this is wrong that a priest [Israel's priests were from the tribe of Levi – a Levite] should have a concubine, not his wife, just a concubine. This is following really the pagan practices of

the people that were around him and even the priest. ...They had a live-in relationship; living together without marriage."

In the above quote, Smith reduces their relationship to one of 'just living together". However, the Hebrew word used to describe her is Ishshah. This concubine would have been at the level of an additional wife, as was the custom of the time. Nothing is recorded in the Old Testament where God condemned men for having concubines. These men's households (Abraham, David, Solomon) were blessed financially and they were successful in God's eyes and for His purposes. Scholars can't adequately explain why God would allow men to have concubines while scripture simultaneously forbids adultery. Is having a concubine wrong? There is no biblical statement to condemn it. The interpretive problem within this issue of concubinage lies within our understanding of the word, adultery. Adultery is typically viewed from a sexual and marital perspective instead of a commitment perspective like the concept of idolatry. Was it God's intention for a man to have one wife? It does not appear that it mattered. There were instances where a man chose to have one wife; others decided to have more than one wife. In our larger contemporary society, some men decide to have multiple girlfriends (married or not), other men are happily and completely monogamous.

Genesis 2:24 explains that male and female would procreate. As typical with the character of God, He was and is concerned with man's commitment, not an institution nor his religion. He wants to know if we are going to do what we said we were going to do. God wants man to remain committed to the woman he chooses. The

Bible compares Israel and God's relationship to that of a marriage. God stated that He is a jealous God and will have no other gods before Him, meaning Israel could only have one God-husband. However, there is no explicit instruction or command in scripture where a man could only have one wife. This is an interpretive assumption based on the union of Adam and Eve.

When Jesus would make references to Old Testament scripture in the Gospels, He would usually expand on the passage to make a point. In Matthew 5:28, Jesus expands the commandment, 'Do not commit adultery.' "But I say to you that whoever looks at a woman to lust for her has *already committed adultery* with her in his heart." [Italics mine] The Greek word for woman in this verse is *gyne*. Gyne means any woman, a betrothed woman or someone's wife. This same word is translated as wife a few verses later in verse 32. Since the context of the passage is the same, why is a different English word used? Gyne is translated woman in verse 28, but as wife in verse 32. A different word should not be used here. We have learned that adultery in the Old Testament is defined as taking someone else's wife. In this New Testament verse, Jesus is quoting the Old Testament passage. Jesus is basically saying, not only should you honor the covenant with your own wife, but if you lust in your heart after another man's wife, you have already committed adultery by breaking covenant with your own wife.

When Jesus is challenged on the issue of divorce in Matthew 19, He does not expand on His quotation of Genesis 2:24. He merely explains it. "So then, they are no longer two but one flesh. Therefore what God has joined together, let not man separate."[55]

This phrase, 'let not man separate', has been interpreted to mean 'do not divorce'. It actually is exhorting men to not "put away" their wives. It is also assumed that the phrase implies that marriage is between only one man and one woman. The pattern of polygamy found throughout the Old Testament, without judgment or criticism from God, is an indication that either God did not define or require marriage to solely be between one man and one woman; or the type of union was not as important as the commitment within the union. When Jesus made his reference to this passage, He did not comment or correct the past marriage patterns that were obviously present in the Torah, the Old Testament portion that He would have read. If the pattern was as critical as the commitment, this would have been the context and time for Jesus to mention it. However, He did not. Does this mean that monogamy is wrong or not desired? No. It does mean that God expects for a man to remain committed to and provide for the spouse and family he has established.

New Testament Marriage

The common expression of marriage in the New Testament is that of monogamy, one man and one woman. One reason men in the Old Testament had multiple wives was based on economics. They lived in an agrarian society. The larger families provided more workers. The more workers they had the wealthier the family could become. We do not find many families with these numbers in the New Testament; neither do we see numerous wives. Polygamy was an economic choice and practiced by the very wealthy. The majority of 'common' people practiced monogamy as they could not afford to do otherwise.

In First Timothy 3, Paul indirectly mentions polygamy in his list of qualifications for a bishop and deacon. In this list, Paul is stating that a leader must have moral integrity. He states that bishops and deacons must be "the husband of one wife". The only way a man could be the husband of more than one wife if he were a widower, a divorcé or a polygamist. Of these three social positions, which would be lacking in moral integrity? It would be illogical for a widower to be excluded from church leadership as there is nothing immoral about one's spouse dying. The spouse's death would render him *unmarried*. Being divorced could present a problem in leadership, especially if the break up was new. However, Jesus clarified in Matthew 19 that divorce is allowable when sexual immorality was present. If his spouse was unfaithful, then he would be free to divorce. In the contemporary church, many leaders, male and female have been divorced, while being Christians, without the exclusion of sexual infidelity. Many of us know some of these leaders personally, as some of them are our pastors, bible study teachers and deacons. The only option left that Paul could be referring to is polygamy. In contemporary society and culture, polygamy would not serve the same purpose that it did in ancient Israel or New Testament times. Families are typically smaller today. We are well beyond the agrarian and industrial ages. Family owned businesses, as well as, large corporations employ mostly 'non-relatives' for their workforce. In addition to being illegal in America, polygamy is nearly obsolete. However, we do not find a specific prohibition of polygamy in either testament for the general population. Paul's qualification for monogamy applied to church leadership.

What we do find, within the context of marriage, is the provision of commitment and sexual pleasure. Jesus' discussion on divorce in the book of Matthew confirms the need for commitment. In First Corinthians, Paul says that a husband and a wife owe a 'sexual kindness' to each other and that neither should rob the other one. When the 'debt' is paid often and on time, sexual immorality is preventable.[56] Marriage, obviously, had a purpose in procreation as well.

Once the 'church fathers' came on the scene in the 2nd century, the social construct of marriage and views on marital intercourse began to shift. Christian views on marriage and fidelity varied among scholars. Some early Christian writers, such as Augustine, Justin Martyr, Athenagoras and Clement of Alexandria believed that procreation was the sole purpose of sex within a marriage. This belief is still held by some in the Catholic Church and even among some contemporary Christians. As various Old Testament passages and the Apostle Paul in the New Testament have taught, the purpose of marriage is for procreation **and** sexual pleasure.

Augustine was one of the prominent church fathers of Christianity. His teachings have influenced how modern day Christians view the broader issues of creation, salvation, sin, and the Church. Not only has Augustine's interpretation of scripture and teachings influenced the church's views about marriage, the life he lived and his personal choices also made a direct impact on modern

Christian marriage. Augustine wrote a great deal about his personal struggles with lust. He had sexual relationships and fathered a child, outside of marriage, before he converted to Christianity. It has been suggested that he had at least one homosexual relationship based on his description of a male companion in his book, Confessions. Augustine's experience with pre-marital sex, lust and marriage distorted his view of sex within marriage. Augustine wrote,

> "Marital intercourse for the sake of procreation has no fault attached to it, but for the satisfying of lust, even with one's husband or wife, for the faith of the bed, is venially sinful; but adultery or fornication is mortally sinful. Moreover, continence from all intercourse is even better than marital intercourse itself, even if it takes place for the sake of procreation. But even though continence is better, to pay the dues of marriage is no crime, but to demand it beyond the necessity of procreation is a venial sin, although fornication and adultery are mortally sinful."[57]

He believed that sex was for the sole purpose of procreation and that abstaining from all sex was better than having sex, even within a marital context. He believed that sex between married partners was lustful on par with lusting after someone else's spouse. This belief is contrary to the teachings of scripture. Furthermore, it has influenced the practical application of marriage within the Christian church. For Augustine, marriage and its 'lust' was a hindrance. He would have preferred to remain unmarried, like Apostle Paul, but he could not contain his sexual desires.

> "But I was still tightly bound by the love of women; nor did the apostle forbid me to marry, although he

exhorted me to something better, wishing earnestly
that all men were as he himself was. But I was weak
and chose the easier way, and for this single reason
my whole life was one of inner turbulence and
listless indecision, because from so many influences
I was compelled--even though unwilling--to agree to
a married life which bound me hand and foot. I had
heard from the mouth of Truth that 'there are
eunuchs who have made themselves eunuchs for
the Kingdom of Heaven's sake' but, said he, 'He
that is able to receive it, let him receive it.' "[58]

Augustine believed that singleness was better and marriage
was 'taking the easy way out'. His stringent position on marriage and
sexual relations did not come solely from scripture, but was biased,
resulting from Augustine's own experience and his interpretation of
Apostle Paul's experience. The Bible clearly teaches that sex is not
just a means for conception. It is an expression of love as well as the
meeting of physical desires. God purposely created us to have sex.
Sex is a gift! It appears that even the church fathers misunderstood
and misapplied the scriptures in this regard. What other scriptures
and concepts have been misinterpreted?

The Apostle Paul had a similar outlook on marriage. He
continues a discussion on marriage in First Corinthians 7. Paul was
responding to a letter that he had previously received from the
Corinthian church. This original letter has been lost in antiquity. We
do not know specifically what questions or concerns Paul was
addressing, however he starts out with his opinion in verse 1. "It is
good for a man not to touch a woman." This is a strong
introductory statement for a teaching on marriage. Paul figured if
men did not touch women (i.e. have, or get close enough to have,

sexual intercourse), they would not be encumbered by the personal responsibilities and sexual desires of marriage. He continues in the next verse about the prevention of illegal sexual intercourse (i.e. adultery). He says in verse 2, 'husbands get your *own* wife and wives get your *own* husband.' [Italics mine] The Greek word *heautou* means to himself or themselves. The implication of the verse is to "get a wife unto himself". A *slang* translation would be "get your *own self* a husband". Paul phrases his statement this way because the true essence of adultery is to have sex with someone else's spouse. He admonishes them to *get your own*!

Here are some simple truths we have learned about marriage. It is clear that the scriptures teach that sex is for pleasure. The critical element in a marital relationship is commitment. Scripture does not prohibit polygamy. Some have tried to say that King David's repentance in 2 Samuel 12 was for adultery and polygamy. It was not. We do not find anyone in the Old Testament repenting for having more than one wife. David repented for *taking* another man's wife away from him and killing him by the sword of his enemy. This is why David's punishment was that "the sword shall never depart from your house" and God "will take your *wives*...and give them to your neighbors." If God were condemning polygamy, He would have contradicted Himself in this statement. At this point, David was already married to Ahinoam, Abigail, Maach, Haggith, Abital, Eglah and Michal. Is this a picture of traditional marriage from Genesis 2:24? Not at all.

Given the biased opinions and teachings on the marriage of these two renowned biblical figures (Apostle Paul and St. Augustine), is it not possible that the scriptures have been misunderstood and misapplied as it relates to homosexuality and homosexual relationships as well?

C H A P T E R   1 0
New Testament Homosexuality

Does the Bible really condemn homosexuality in the New Testament? The answer to this question remains to be seen. The Bible was not originally written in English. This fact has been stated before, but sometimes the Bible is read at face value as if its original language was English. Some ancient Hebrew and Greek words had multiple meanings like some English words today. The English word *love* is a prime example. In order to fully understand what is meant by the usage of the word *love* in a sentence, an overall context must be established. Here is an example:

> I wrote an old friend a letter. This friend knows me very well. The context of the letter should be crystal clear to him. It contained the following sentence:
>
> *I love Peaches.*
>
> I am talking about fruit, right? Maybe. If I add the following question before the sentence, it will clarify that point.
>
> *What kind of fruit do I like most? I love Peaches.*
> This explains my strong affinity for peaches. What if I don't have the preceding question, but instead have the following statement:

I love Peaches. She has always been there for me.
Now the context has completely changed. I am not talking about fruit, but some type of relationship. It is probably with someone with a nickname, since 'Peaches' is not a traditional name. Maybe it's my sister or a female friend. What happens, when I add this statement?

I love Peaches. She has always been there for me.
Remember when she chased that burglar away from my car?

Now it is clear that I am talking about my love and appreciation for my dog (or aggressively bold cat!). This is called context. Context is critical for understanding the meaning of words, especially across time periods and cultures. What if I replace the last sentence with the following?

I love Peaches. She has always been there for me.
And I'm going to be there for her too.
I asked her to marry me last night and she said yes!
With this change, I am still talking about a relationship, but a totally different type. Instead of a relationship between me and my sister or my dog, it is one between me and my fiancée. Since I am talking about relationships, is the context of the last two scenarios identical? They both talk about my love for Peaches. However, they are not identical because the type of love I have for my dog is different than that for my fiancée. Without these clarifying sentences, no one reading this letter would understand what I am talking

about. Could you imagine someone reading it 1,000 years from now? The only way they could understand the meaning is with all of the clarifying sentences. If some sentences were missing, the reader would need some other letters written by me (to possibly understand my style of writing and frame of reference) or some letters written about me to gain insight on what I may have been trying to say. The same context is needed when reading and understanding the Bible.

This issue of context is of the utmost importance when dealing with biblical interpretation. Within it, context uses elements of history, culture, geography and social norms to bring about understanding and definition. It is critical to interpreting the meaning and relevance of any passage of scripture for modern times.

In the next sections on Romans 1 and First Corinthians 6, I will point out how certain biblical passages have been misinterpreted because the original context was misunderstood or ignored. In this chapter, I review each of the scriptures that are commonly used to make a reference to homosexuality.

Romans 1:18 - 32

For the wrath of God is revealed from heaven against all ungodliness and unrighteousness of men, who suppress the truth in unrighteousness, because what may be known of God is manifest in them, for God has shown it to them. For since the creation of the world His invisible attributes are clearly seen, being understood by the things that are made, even His eternal power and Godhead, so that they are without excuse, because, although they knew God, they did not glorify Him as

God, nor were thankful, but became futile in their thoughts, and their foolish hearts were darkened. Professing to be wise, they became fools, and changed the glory of the incorruptible God into an *image* made like corruptible man--and birds and four-footed animals and creeping things. Therefore God also gave them up to uncleanness, in the lusts of their hearts, to dishonor their bodies among themselves, who exchanged the truth of God for the lie, and worshiped and served the *creature* rather than the Creator, who is blessed forever. Amen.
For this reason God gave them up to vile passions. For even their women exchanged the natural use for what is against nature. Likewise also the men, leaving the natural use of the woman, burned in their lust for one another, men with men committing what is shameful, and receiving in themselves the penalty of their error which was due. And even as they did not like to retain God in their knowledge, God gave them over to a debased mind, to do those things which are not fitting; being filled with all unrighteousness, sexual immorality, wickedness, covetousness, maliciousness; full of envy, murder, strife, deceit, evil-mindedness; they are whisperers, backbiters, haters of God, violent, proud, boasters, inventors of evil things, disobedient to parents, undiscerning, untrustworthy, unloving, unforgiving, unmerciful; who, knowing the righteous judgment of God, that those who practice such things are deserving of death, not only do the same but also approve of those who practice them. (Italics mine)

This first chapter of Romans contains the most controversial passage of scripture regarding homosexuality. Its message appears to be a clear and definitive prohibition of all same sex expression. All same sex expression is not equal just like all opposite sex expression is not equal. There are heterosexual activities that are prohibited. There are prohibitions on certain types of homosexual behavior as well. As with all scripture, consistent hermeneutical principles need to be applied to determine how the scripture can be interpreted for our modern culture. The text recorded in Chapter 1 needs to be interpreted in light of the message of the entire book of Romans as well as the rest of the Bible. This mode of interpretation follows context and the hermeneutical "agreement" principle where no passage will contradict another. In other words, a meaning of a passage is understood in the context of its relation to other passages as well as the Bible as a whole. What message was Paul trying to convey in the book of Romans? At the time of the writing of his letter to the Roman church, he had not yet visited Rome. During this time, he was residing in a city called Corinth. The establishment of the Christian Church at Rome was possibly a result of his overall global ministry, but Paul did not directly establish this church. One of Paul's goals for the Roman letter was to establish doctrine for its members. Paul had done the same thing for the church in Corinth, however in person. After establishing the doctrine for the Corinthian church, he then stayed in Corinth for 18 months "teaching the Word of God." [59] He did not have this same privilege with the Romans. In his letter, he provided the Romans with the basic doctrine of redemption in Christ for Jews and Gentiles (non-Jews). This makes up the central theme of Romans. <u>Paul's intention was **not** to "address specific local problems" because he had not visited the church yet. [60] Since this was not Paul's goal, the book of Romans cannot be read from this perspective.</u> He taught that "God is righteous…even though all men are sinful and even though believers may not fully live in a way consistent with God's righteousness."[61] Furthermore, he believed that Christians should "imitate the faith of Abraham, rejoice in our representation by Christ, grow in daily death to sin and walk according to the Spirit each moment."[62] This is how the overall book of Romans applies to the believer today.

<u>Romans, Chapter 1</u>

Chapter 1 of Romans is about the power of the gospel for *all* people and how humanity in general suppressed the revelation of God. In his letter to the Romans, Paul was influenced by his current circumstances and surroundings. He was not living in Rome, but Corinth, a city known for its extreme sexual immorality, idolatry and prostitution. He wanted to establish a message that has been the central theme of the entire Bible. It can be found in these two scripture passages.

> "Hear, O Israel: The LORD our God, the LORD is one! You shall love the LORD your God with all your heart, with all your soul, and with all your strength."[63]
> "You shall have no other gods before Me."[64]

Paul's message in the book of Romans was that no other god was to be worshipped by the Jewish and Gentile believers other than Jehovah God. In other words, do not commit idolatry.

In the first 17 verses of this book, the word *faith* (Gk. *Pistis*) appears five times. The word means to have a strong conviction or belief that Jesus Christ is the Messiah. This was an important message to preach to the Jewish inhabitants of Rome. Paul wanted them to know that Jesus is God, he is the Messiah they were waiting for and again, no other god is to be worshipped.

However, he lived around the 'unconverted' Corinthians and they worshipped Aphrodite, the goddess of love. Their worship practices involved people engaging in ritualistic sex with male and female prostitutes in their temples. This specific form of idolatry was commonplace in Corinth. Paul discusses idolatry from a broader perspective in verse 23-25. He states that *mankind*, his subject mentioned in verse 18, "changed the glory of the incorruptible God into an *image*…"[65] Here is a biblical definition of idolatry. It is "a major sin in the Abrahamic religions regarding *image*. It is usually defined as worship of any *cult image, idea, or object*, as opposed to the worship of God." [Italics mine.][66] Paul continues in verse 24-25,

> "Therefore [because of the idolatry mentioned in the previous verse], God also gave them up to uncleanness, in the lusts of their heart, to dishonor their bodies among themselves, who exchanged *the truth* of God for *the lie*, and worshipped and served the creature rather than the Creator, who is blessed forever. Amen." [Italics mine]

In this passage, it is important to know what was *the truth* and *the lie* to which Paul referred? The *truth* is found in verse 16, "…it is the power of God to salvation for everyone who believes…" The *lie* was mankind's rejection of God through idolatrous behaviors as demonstrated by the Romans and Corinthians' pagan worship at the temple of Aphrodite. These acts of idolatry defined their belief as being opposite of *the truth* found in verse 16. Instead of worshipping God, the Greco-Roman society chose to worship Aphrodite. Their method of worship was through ritualistic sexual acts. This example at Rome is a *representation* of mankind's overall participation in idolatrous acts throughout biblical history. Verses 19-21 explain that the *truth* had already been revealed to mankind, but it was exchanged for something else, in this case what was desired at Aphrodite's altar.

Paul described to the Romans how, mankind as a whole, is idolatrous. Because the passage sounds so similar to the pagan temple worship that occurred in Corinth, it must have been hard for him to separate himself from his current surroundings. The idolatry of the Corinthians apparently influenced his writings to the Romans, the audience of this letter. Paul actually used his surroundings to help illustrate his points. He becomes more specific as he continues in verses 26-27, beginning with "For this reason..." Paul wanted to make clear his topic of idolatry, so that the Romans would understand that no other God was to be worshipped. Idolatry is such a broad concept, Paul needed to help the Romans make a connection to it, so he spoke of specific idolatrous behavior within the Greco-Roman culture. He states "God gave them up to vile passions (disgraceful passionate deeds in Greek)". What were the disgraceful passionate deeds? The idolatrous practices were the disgraceful passionate deeds. "Gave them up" is a phrase unique to idolatry and the impure motives behind it.[67] It is the same phrase that Luke used in Acts 7:42, when he described God's response to the Israelites when they made the golden calf (idol) instead of waiting on Moses to bring the word of God.[68] The Romans' idolatrous behavior is clear up to this point. However, this is the point in the passage where eisegesis (reading a pre-established interpretation into the passage) begins and clarity wanes. Upon arriving at the word "passions", many Bible readers and scholars have abandoned the broad context of the passage (idolatry and the suppressed revelation of God) and moved to a different and specific teaching -- homosexuality. It is clear from the words in the text that a type of homosexual activity is being described; however the passage is not a condemnation of homosexual orientation or homosexuality in and of itself. It is a condemnation of idolatry in the form of homosexual and heterosexual sexual activity in pagan worship. Homosexual activity is when two persons of the same gender engage in a sexual exchange or interaction. This does not necessarily take into consideration their sexual orientation or primary sexual attraction. Homosexual orientation is when a person is physically and/or emotionally attracted to the same gender, whether they engage in sexual activity or not. Sexual experience or activity is not required to be homosexually oriented. Some heterosexual people can and do participate in homosexual activity for various reasons. This is called situational homosexuality. In contemporary society, situational homosexuality can be found within the prison system. Most incarcerated men are heterosexual as is the majority of the world's population. These incarcerated men engage in homosexual behaviors for lack of female companionship; release of sexual tension and/or reasons related to control, commodity, power and abuse. Many of these men return to heterosexuality upon leaving the prison system. Situational homosexuality is also a part of the prostitution trade. Individuals who engage in prostitution either choose to or are forced into this exploitive profession. They may find themselves in dire straits and they see this activity as their only way of survival. Some of these prostitutes are heterosexual men who are propositioned by homosexual customers. For the prostitute, sex is a job. Many will take on any paying customer, especially if drug dependence is a factor. The pornography industry is no different. It contains heterosexual male actors/models who will participate in homosexual activity because the pay is better than in heterosexual pornography. This is known as 'gay for pay'. For them, the financial reward is the sole appeal. They find themselves in a situation where engaging in homosexual activity is beneficial for them in a non-sexual way. They are otherwise heterosexual. The pornography industry is full of heterosexual women who engage in lesbian activity for pay. The homosexual activity Paul was referring to was the sexual activity males were having with the male prostitutes at the temple of Aphrodite. These male 'worshippers' were both heterosexual and homosexual. The female 'worshippers' were engaging in these same behaviors. In addition, there was another male homosexual activity that occurred in their society called pederasty. I will discuss pederasty later in this section.

The end of Romans 1:27 teaches that, as a result of mankind's idolatry, they received "the penalty of their error which was due." Some people would say this penalty refers to things like venereal diseases or HIV. This is understandable as the phrase is connected to the sexual context of the first part of verse 27. However, the penalty must also be connected to mankind's overall idolatry as that is the true subject at hand. The text interprets itself and explains what the penalty is. <u>The penalty is the list described in verses 28-32.</u> These verses can be paraphrased from the original Greek this way: *Even after that, they did not recognize that what they were worshipping was not genuine [idols], nor did they have the correct or precise knowledge of God. So God gave them over to the power of that which does not*

prove itself as it ought (a debased mind), to do things that don't fit. The things
that *don't fit* are listed in verses 28-31.

> "...to do those things which are not fitting; being filled with all
> unrighteousness, **sexual immorality**, wickedness,
> covetousness, maliciousness; full of envy, murder, strife,
> deceit, evil-mindedness; they are whisperers, backbiters, haters
> of God, violent, proud, boasters, inventors of evil things,
> disobedient to parents, undiscerning, untrustworthy, unloving,
> unforgiving, unmerciful"

Interestingly, the second 'thing' mentioned in the list is the phrase
"sexual immorality". If verse 27 is a description of an *immoral* sexual
practice (versus an *idolatrous* sexual practice), why would 'sexual
immorality' need to be mentioned as a penalty for itself? In other
words, if Paul is solely condemning 'sexual immorality' in verses 24-
27, how is 'sexual immorality' a penalty for… 'sexual immorality' in
verse 29? The answer to this question is not found in the intention
of Paul's message as much as in how this verse was translated into
English.

There are two translation tools widely used by Bible scholars
in order to gain a clear understanding of scripture. They are versions
or translations of the Bible, written in Greek, that scholars use when
translating a version into the English language. As of this writing,
these tools are the *Nestle-Aland Greek New Testament (27th edition)* and
United Bibles Societies' Greek New Testament (3rd edition)[69]. Although, the
New King James Version of the Bible contains the words "sexual
immorality" in verse 29, both of these Greek translations of the
Bible omit them. Their purposeful omission is probably due to the
confusion that would be caused by their seemingly redundancy
regarding the usage of the words, sexual immorality. However, when

the context of the behavior described in verse 27 is properly understood as the practice of idolatry, the inclusion of 'sexual immorality' in verse 29 is no longer redundant. The New King James Version is correct. Thus, there is no need to omit it. This is because sexual immorality and idolatry are two related, but distinct ideas. Notice that idolatry is not mentioned repetitiously in the list of penalties either. Its absence is appropriate, given that the context of the entire passage is idolatry. It would not make grammatical sense to repeat it. Romans 1 is about idolatry, not homosexuality. Additional examples of Paul's strong stance against idolatry can be found in Acts 17:16-31. In First Corinthians 10:7-8, he also links idolatry to sexual immorality when he references Numbers 25:9 in this passage.

Natural Use of Women

Another concern with the Romans 1 passage is the usage of the word 'natural' in verse 26 & 27. During this ancient biblical period, women were seen as *useful* when they were able to bear children. The Greek word for use is *chresis* which means the sexual use of a woman. In the chapter on Old Testament Homosexuality, I discussed the Hebrew words *Piylegesh* and *Ishshah* which were sometimes used interchangeably for a man's wife or his concubine. Women (*Piylegesh* or *Ishshah*) were used for a man's sexual pleasure and to bear his children. Sexual intercourse and childbearing was a 'natural use' for a woman, as mentioned in verse 26. The word, *use*, is an interesting choice but not a surprising one. The phrasing of this verse is a bit objectifying of women, as their purpose was viewed as one of *service*. If one wanted to describe any type of passionate sexual behavior, even between two lesbians, 'use' would be an illogical choice. However, I believe Paul used the word intentionally. Although the Apostle Paul would have preferred people to remain unmarried like himself, in First Corinthians, he describes marital sex as one of pleasure and not just procreation. He also understood the culture of his audience, especially the Jewish men who historically viewed women as property, thus having sex with them would be the use of their property.[70] For the most part, sexual activity is no longer viewed this way. What was Paul's intention with the phrase 'natural use' in relation to the women? It cannot be a reference to lesbianism because the text does not say they left their natural use and turned to each other, as it is so often misread. Most likely, he was distinguishing the exploitation of the body by Aphrodite's prostitutes versus sexual intercourse and childbearing in a marriage. The body's natural use is not for idolatrous practices (i.e. pagan temple worship). In First Corinthians, Paul says the opposite; that our bodies are for the Lord's use.

The same sex encounter mentioned in the New King James Version of verse 27, states, "men with men committing that which is shameful". Two Greek words are used to describe this exchange: *Katergazomai* (committing in English) means to perform, accomplish, or achieve something; and *Aschemosune* (shameful in English) means an unseemly or shameful deed due to one being naked. The definitions of these terms do not render a context of sexual *expression*, but rather a sexual *practice*. To clarify, making love to your spouse is a sexual expression. Having sex with a different partner each week is a sexual practice. In the practice of idolatry, one is attempting to accomplish the goal of pleasing or obeying the deity being worshipped. The 'worshipper' is also attempting to gain favor from the deity that is the object of his worship. If successful, this is an accomplishment. Why did Paul use a term denoting that 'men with men' was a sexual accomplishment versus a sexual expression? This question must be asked if you believe the verse is describing homosexuality or homosexual relationships in general. You must address homosexuality as an orientation and homosexual relationships separately because every heterosexual act mentioned in scripture is not in the context of a relationship. So, what about the sexual act of homosexuality rendered it shameful? More definitive terms could have been used, if Paul's intent was to describe same sex behavior that is distinct from idolatry. The Greek term *ginosko* (English translation is *know*) was a word used to describe sexual intercourse like the Hebrew word, yada (also translated *know*). Paul did not use this word. It is a historical fact that homosexuality existed within the Greco-Roman society. However, homosexuality, in and of itself, is not an idolatrous act. If so, who or what is being worshipped in the place of God? If the sexual expression between two men or two women is considered 'worshipping the created thing' as opposed to the Creator[71], then heterosexuality would be the same type of idolatrous worship. The Greek word for 'created thing' is *Ktisis*. It means anything that is created, be it a person, an object or an established system. Given the fact that the overall context of the book of Romans is idolatry, the Ktisis (created thing) referenced in verse 24 must be an idol (like Aphrodite) or the system of idolatry as a whole, but not individual persons.

In the upcoming section on First Corinthians 6:9, I discuss a pagan practice that existed among the Romans and Greeks called *pederasty*. In a simple definition, pederasty is the exploitation of young boys by older men, in which they seduce the boys into a sexual relationship. In the culture of the times, the older men who would engage in this behavior were not solely homosexual. In many instances, they were heterosexual married men. These men had wives as well as male and female 'sexual servants'. (Sexual servants were common in ancient Israel as well.) The fact that these men were married lends credence to the fact that sexuality is fluid. All people do not fit into an exclusive heterosexual or exclusive homosexual box. Although individuals may be close to one end of the spectrum, most people fall somewhere in the middle. In the Corinthian passage, the young male servants were described as being soft like women. When Paul talked about "men with men" in Romans 1:27, he specifically used the word, Arsen, which means "a male", not a man. The difference between using a term for male versus man is an important one. Traditionally, when we read the Romans text, we envision *adult men* engaging in this behavior with other adult men. The correct usage of Arsen as 'male', gives a clear picture of the activity in question. I will get to that in a moment. If Paul was intentionally and only speaking about adult men, he would have used the term aner. Later, in Romans 7:3, Paul discusses the subjects of marriage and adultery. He uses the term aner in the passage. "So then, if, while her husband lives, she marries another man (aner), she will be called an adulteress..." Aner is a Greek word for a man which is distinguished from a boy.[72] This word is also used to describe a man in a sexual context. An *Aner* could not be a boy. An *Arsen* could be a boy or a man. Thus the usage of aner is appropriate in Romans 7 because adult men get married, have sex and can commit adultery. However, in chapter 1 of the same letter, Paul uses a term that is used to describe males as a gender (Arsen). Why would he make that distinction if it were not intentional? Remember the book of Romans is one large letter addressed to a single group. Paul's word usage was intentional because he was discussing males in two different age groups in chapter 1 and an adult man in chapter 7. If a reader were unaware of the type of idolatry (use of temple prostitutes in worship) existed in Greco-Roman society, then reading the Greek term *Arsen* (male) would not stand out. However, if it were understood that the practice of pederasty existed as well as male temple prostitution, then a term that describes the male gender versus adult males would be necessary in the overall discussion of idolatry.

There are a lot of slight nuances, like this one, that have been overlooked when certain scriptures are interpreted. These differences do not appear to hold much significance when an interpretation has **already** been applied to a passage. When you look at the context of the book of Romans, Paul's other writings and the environments in which Paul resided, a condemnation of homosexuality is not as apparent as traditionally taught. Although it was commonplace in the society in which they lived, what becomes apparent is that the practice of pederasty and temple prostitution was

not a 'natural' use of another male. <u>What is even more important is
that Paul was not condemning the Romans for any specific behavior.</u>
Paul had never been to Rome and had not met these people. He was
sharing that the revealed gospel brings righteousness – the power of
God for the salvation of everyone who **believes**. He continues with
God's revealed anger towards the godlessness and wickedness of
men who suppress the truth. This is God's overall eternal anger
towards sin; not any anger towards the Romans. If Paul were
specifically condemning these Roman men, it would have been for
leaving their sexual relationships with their wives and engaging in
these common, but pagan practices.

First Corinthians 6:9

> Do you not know that the unrighteous will not inherit the
> kingdom of God? Do not be deceived. Neither fornicators,
> nor idolaters, nor adulterers, nor homosexuals, nor sodomites,
> nor thieves, nor covetous, nor drunkards, nor revilers, nor
> extortioners will inherit the kingdom of God.

*(In order to distinguish God's people from the pagan residents, in this section I
will refer to God's people as Corinthian believers and the unbelievers as
Corinthian residents.)*

We read the English word homosexual here, however, this
verse in First Corinthians 6 is not a condemnation of homosexuality.
Again, it is a condemnation of idolatry, which must be understood in
the context of the entire passage. What is the context of the sixth
chapter of First Corinthians? Chapter 6 is a continuation of a

thought from Chapter 5. Chapter 5 talks about how the sexual immorality of an individual affects the entire body of Christian believers. The chapter ends with the admonishment of Christians to not judge those on the "outside" (non-Christians) because that is God's job. However, Paul was instructing the Corinthian church leaders to *judge* those on the "inside" (Christian believers). The word judge means to pronounce an opinion of right and wrong. It is God's job to pronounce who is right or wrong in relation to sin and salvation (those on the outside) because He is the only one who truly knows. As church leaders, Paul was saying it is their responsibility to pronounce who is right or wrong within the church community regarding sin, such as the man who had sex with his father's wife. In chapter 6, Paul continues with instructions on how believers are to act and interact with each other, specifically in regards to legal matters. Believers are not to allow unbelievers to make legal judgments on their behalf.[73] Paul observed that the Corinthian believers would rather "do wrong and cheat" their own brothers, by using 'outside' counsel instead of going to a fellow Christian. Paul's letter to the Corinthian believers was one of instruction. This letter was not some theoretical discourse, but had true and current application for the readers. Paul did not want the Corinthian believers to take their private matters to the 'outside' residents of Corinth. He heard about the type of people the Corinthian *residents* were and the beliefs that drove their immoral behavior. They were not examples of how God wanted His people to behave.

When we arrive at verse 9 of First Corinthians chapter 6, Paul does not start a new thought. He continues from the previous thought by educating the believers that those people on the "outside" were unrighteous and not partakers in the rulership of God (Kingdom of God). Paul then provides a list of the types of people who will not receive an inheritance that comes from being in God's kingdom. Before looking at the list in verse 9 & 10, we must keep in mind the context of chapter five and six. Paul is talking about the Corinthian residents being a sexually immoral people who are extortioners, idolatrous and abusive. He tells the Corinthian believers not to associate with them.[74] Then Paul reminds some of them that they came from the same community, as some converted to Christianity and joined the Corinthian church. They were once just like the unbelieving Corinthians, but God had separated them and was in the process of making them a different type of people.[75]

In verses 9 & 10 of the New King James version, Paul gives two distinctions of the Corinthian people. The description of one group is clear. The other group's description presents some theological and translation problems. In verse 10, Paul says they are thieves, covetous, drunks, rioters and extortioners; basically they are irresponsible and not trustworthy. In verse 9, they are fornicators, idolaters, adulterers, homosexuals and sodomites. One of the two main problems in verse 9 is that there are two Greek words used in this verse that do not seem to fit within the context, so it makes them difficult to translate. They are Malakos and Arsenokoites. Throughout the entire Bible, Arsenokoites only appears in one other passage. Malakos appears in two gospel accounts in the same context, *unrelated* to its supposed meaning in First Corinthians or sexuality in general.

The second problem is the way contemporary bible scholars have attempted to translate these two words, taking them out of the context of this passage and chapter. In the New King James version, there are 5 words in verse 9 that must be understood in their correct English translation in order for the context of this passage to be cohesive and fit within the context of the rest of the chapter. We will take an in-depth look at each of these words and their usage outside of this passage and outside of the Bible, in order to gain a clear meaning of them. Before we do that, let's take a brief look at the context of the rest of chapter six.

First Corinthians 6:12-13

"All things are lawful for me, but all things are not helpful. All things are lawful for me, but I will not be brought under the power of any. Foods for the stomach and the stomach for foods, but God will destroy both it and them. Now the body is not for sexual immorality but for the Lord, and the Lord for the body."

Verses 12-13 discuss the importance of our body in the experience of worshipping God. We cannot just worship God with our spirits. We complete our expression of worship as it is acted out through our body. Paul was making this statement as a point of education and confirmation. Some of the new Corinthian believers may have been unaware or confused on this point. Gnosticism was a widely followed religious movement which basically elevated knowledge above faith. Gnostics placed a strong emphasis on the divine where the body was *less important* in worship. Therefore, some Gnostics were known for feeding whatever bodily desires would arise in them. Their sole belief in the importance of the spirit enabled them to be very sexually indulgent. In verse 13, Paul was clarifying the difference between hunger urges and sexual urges. Although food is made to nourish the body and the body in turn digests the food to obtain the nutrients, the body was not intended for illicit or forbidden sexual activity. The purpose for sexual relations is to have an intimate connection with your partner, on a level that does not exist in other relationships. Sex provides knowledge of another person at the level of their soul. Sex provides a spiritual connection between two people. This experience should not be taken lightly.

Paul tells the Corinthians that their **bodies** are a part of Christ. Romans 6:17 teaches us that we are 'firmly joined or glued to" Christ. Salvation is a relationship between Christ and the Christian Church where the people, collectively, make up His body.[76] In verse 15 of First Corinthians, Paul asks the Corinthian believers a rhetorical question. Should you take your bodies that are joined to Christ and join them with a prostitute? Remember the context of chapter six is the idolatrous and immoral practices of the Corinthian residents acted out through ritual sex acts. Paul was making a distinction between the character of the unbelieving Corinthians and the believing Corinthians. When Paul refers to joining with a prostitute, he is referencing the pagan practice of the Corinthian residents that some of the new believers were accustomed to participating in. He wanted to prevent the new believers from combining pagan worship practices with Christian worship practices. Paul was referring to the pagan worship of the goddess, Aphrodite. This is the same idolatrous practice that was discussed in the Roman

1 section. Paul was in Corinth when he wrote that letter and was
familiar with the practice. Here, approximately 5 years later, Paul is
addressing the practice directly with the Corinthian believers. The
practice involved 'worshippers' ascending to the temple of Aphrodite
and engaging in sex with temple prostitutes. Even after Aphrodite's
temple was torn down, the idolatrous worship continued throughout
the city. Christian believers were one spirit with God. His spirit
indwelled them. Paul was explaining that when a believer's spirit
connects with a prostitute's spirit, it is the ultimate form of idolatry.
Not simply because they were having sex or even sex with someone
who was not their spouse, but because the prostitute was a physical
representation of the idol deity. In verse 18, Paul says to 'run away'
from this illegal idolatrous sexual practice. When you sin in this
manner you 'miss the mark' of true worship.[77] The Christian
believer's goal was true worship, but true worship could not be
experienced in conjunction with idolatry. Idolatry is a sin against
your spirit – the inside part of your body – as opposed to other sins
which are committed with the outside part of your body. Paul
continues by explaining that the bodies of Corinthian believers **are**
the temples that 'house' God's spirit.[78] There was no need to
'worship' at the temple of Aphrodite. They could correctly worship
their own God within their own temple. The church building is not
where worship takes place. It is where we gather to worship
together. Actually, the only way to truly worship God is with and
through your own body, God's temple.

Sin Lists

Often when Paul listed sins in his writings, he would categorize them or group them together based on some commonality. There were sexual sins, sins of violence, sins of an idolatrous nature or sins based on economic or social injustice. In verses 9 - 10, Paul categorizes sins and sinners as well. In verse 10, he identifies those who commit economic and social injustices as thieves, covetous, drunks, abusers and extortioners. In verse 9, he makes one general reference to those who commit illegal sexual acts and then he identifies those involved in idolatrous behavior being idolaters and adulterers. (Adulterers were often connected to idolaters in the Old and New Testaments. We will look at these terms in more detail.)

Then there are the two terms: Malakos and Arsenokoites. These words seem to be in an odd place in this list. It is unclear if they should either fall within the idolatry group or economic and social injustice group or in a category of their own. If they were to be categorized as sexual sins, they should have been listed immediately after the term 'fornicators'. The order in which sins are listed alone cannot determine the meaning of any word. However, Paul's writing style is something to consider when trying to understand the context of a passage. The definitions, translations and/or usage of these two words outside of the Bible will solidify this point. Since these words have limited usage within the New Testament, it makes sense to look at other ancient writings to see how the words may have been used in other contexts.

Other Usage

The non-canonized New Testament books are authentic writings which were not authorized to become a part of the 66 books of the Christian Bible. The canonized Bible was developed through debate and agreement by religious authorities of the Christian faith. These non-canonized writings were penned by some of the apostles, other noted New Testament figures and those who were in close relationship with them. They are generally known as 'early Christian writings' and also record history during biblical times. These ancient texts shed some light on how words were used in their original Greco-Roman context. Two early Christian writings that contain the words Malakos and Arsenokoites are *I Clement* and the *Acts of John*. A review of the passages in these writings is not an attempt to prove or disprove the validity of homosexuality. The purpose is to understand the meaning of the words by their usage and context.

Arsenokoites

In various versions of the Christian Bible, Arsenokoites has been translated to mean different things, but usually related to some type of sexual activity with men. This word has been translated as homosexual, male prostitute, active (penetrating) male partner in a homosexual encounter and sexual pervert. The various definitions/ translations have been adjusted over the years as it relates to the subject of homosexuality and its impact on society over the same time period. This variation applies to the term Malakos as well. There are two major ways of discovering what Paul's intentions were in using this word. First, we must consider the context of Paul's conversation when he used it. Second, we must look at how this word was used in other contexts. Some have suggested that Paul coined this term by combining the two terms, *arsen* which means 'a male' and *koite* which means 'a place to sleep, bed or a metaphor for having sex'. The translated term means male-bed or male-sex. At face value, it is quite presumptive to say this term means homosexual or infers homosexuality. There is not enough information in the word to understand with whom the male is having sex. The only other place in the New Testament where *Arsenokoites* appears is in I Timothy also written by Paul. In this passage the word is translated as 'sodomite'. A sodomite is known to be a male prostitute. The First Timothy passage further confuses the subject because the translators are saying that an Arsenokoites is not a homosexual, but a male prostitute. The typical reader just assumes that a 'sodomite' is a homosexual based on what they have heard or the connection to the Sodom and Gomorrah story, not the definition of the word. However, if the usage of sodomite is correct, than it fits into the idolatrous culture of the time, as male prostitutes were used at the Temple of Aphrodite. Thus the term is idolatrous and can be grouped with adulterers and idolaters in Paul's group. The passages found in Romans chapter 1, First Corinthians chapter 6 and First Timothy chapter 1 would all have male prostitution in common. If this is not the case, we have to look at other literature of the time to determine a clear usage and meaning of Arsenokoites.

Dale B. Martin, a religious researcher has stated,

"One of the earliest appearances of the word (here the verb, arsenokoitein) occurs in Sibylline Oracle 2.70-77.10. The oracle probably provides an independent use of the word. It occurs in a section listing acts of economic injustice and exploitation; in fact, the editors of the English translation here quoted by J. J. Collins, label the section "On *Justice*": [italics mine]

Translation A
(Never accept in your hand a gift which
derives from unjust deeds.)
Do not steal seeds. Whoever takes for
himself is accursed (to generations of
generations, to the scattering of life.
Do not *arsenokoitein*, do not betray
information, do not murder.) Give one
who has labored his wage. Do not oppress
a poor man. Take heed of your speech.
Keep a secret matter in your heart. (Make
provision for orphans and widows and
those in need.)
Do not be willing to act unjustly, and
therefore do not give leave to one who is
acting unjustly."[79]

In Martin's writing, he is establishing that vice or sin lists in scripture and other Christian writings, provide a greater understanding of the usage and definition of various ancient terms. He espouses since, the *Arsenokoites*-derivative, Arsenokoitein is not listed among any sexual sin, its connotation and/or definition cannot be sexual in nature.

There is a different English translation of this oracle entitled "The Sibylline Oracles translated from the Greek into English by Milton S. Terry [1899]".[80] Martin says that the date of the oracle is uncertain, however, it could have been penned anywhere between the 6th Century BC and 6th Century AD.[81] In the above quote, the word *Arsenokoiten* is written into the translated text. In the English translation by Milton Terry, Arsenokoiten is actually translated this way:

Translation B

A gift proceeding out of unjust deeds
Never receive in hand. Do not steal seed;
Accursed through many generations he
Who took it unto scattering of life.
Indulge not *vile lusts*, slander not, nor kill. [Italics mine]

Milton translates the word Arsenokoiten to mean vile lusts. As far as one can tell, 'vile lusts' is a generic term. It can be used to describe heterosexual or homosexual lust or lust of a non-sexual nature like covetousness. If Arsenokoitein was translated as covetousness, its usage in the context of this passage would definitely make sense. It would read as follows:

"Never receive a gift unjustly, do not steal, do not covet, do not slander, nor kill."

According to editor, James H. Charlesworth, the Sibylline Oracles as translated by J.J. Collins, reads as follows:

Translation A

"(Never accept in your hand a gift which derives from unjust deeds.) Do not steal seeds. Whoever takes for himself is accursed to generations of generations, to the scattering of life. Do not practice homosexuality [¢rsenokoite‹n], do not betray information, do not murder" [82]

When the passage is translated this way, it changes the context in the middle of the thought. Translation A does not appear to be correct.

There is a significant time difference between the release of these two different translations of the oracle containing this word Arsenokoiten; Terry in 1899 and Collins in 1983. Could modern culture have had any bearing on how and why the term in the later translation by J.J. Collins (Translation A) is so specific to homosexuality versus Terry's (Translation B) more general term of vile lusts in the former translation? The Greek passage that is being translated was written approximately 2,000 years ago. The term homosexuality did not exist then. It appears that modern translators were attempting to make these ancient texts say what they already believe them to mean. This *eisegetical* approach of interpretation (reading into the text a preconceived opinion) has also skewed the translations of the Bible.

> "Between the end of the nineteenth and the middle of the twentieth century, therefore, the translation of arsenokoités shifted from being the reference to an action that any man might well perform, regardless of orientation or disorientation, to refer to a "perversion," either an action or a propensity taken to be self-evidently abnormal and diseased. The shift in translation, that is, reflected the invention of the category of "homosexuality" as an abnormal orientation, an invention that occurred in the nineteenth century but gained popular currency only gradually in the twentieth. Furthermore, whereas earlier translations had all taken the term (correctly) to refer to men, the newer translations broadened the reference to include people of either sex who could be diagnosed as suffering from the new modern neurosis of homosexuality. Thorough historical or philological evidence was never adduced to support this shift in translation. The interpretations were prompted not by criteria of historical criticism but by shifts in modern sexual ideology."[83]

Dale G. Martin points out that the definitions for the terms
Arsenokoites and its counterpart Malakos have changed as society
has changed. Arsenokoites formerly was translated as a sexual action
of heterosexual or homosexual men. Now the modern translations
suggest that the word describes a psychosexual abnormality. In an
effort to "keep up" with the church's perception of sexuality, the
meanings of these terms in various Bible translations have shifted
from 'men performing sexual acts with men' (without any specific
sexual orientation implied) to 'homosexual offenders' to 'male
prostitutes' to 'male homosexuals' to 'homosexuality in general'. It is
interesting to note that there is no reference or allusion to female
homosexuality in the entire Bible. The Romans 1 passage says
women 'exchanged the natural use of their bodies' but does not say
they had sex with other women. Lesbianism existed during this time;
however Paul does not mention it. It is clear that Paul is making
reference to Leviticus 20:13 where it condemns a man for having sex
with another man, but nowhere does Leviticus condemn sex
between women. So what was the 'unnatural' practice of the
women? What we do know to have been an unnatural, but widely
accepted practice at the time was prostitution. Prostitution goes
against the natural use for the body.   It is also important to note
that Leviticus 20:15 condemns men for engaging in bestiality and in
20:16, it condemns women for the same act. So, it is clear that there
is no absence of sexual prohibitions for women in scripture.
Lesbianism was not addressed purposefully because no one had a
problem with it. The prohibition of sex between males had a

purpose as well. (See Old Testament Homosexuality for more information.)

In most Bible translations, the two words Arsenokoites and Malakos have remained separate. In a few translations, the words have been combined to 'solidify' their general definition of all things homosexual. I understand attempts at maintaining Christian ethics. However this homosexual issue receives an inordinate amount of attention, as opposed to other virtues that seem to receive less attention, like caring for widows and orphans or heterosexual fidelity and purity. The latter is definitely preached upon, but a practical demonstration of addressing the behavior (i.e. protests and picketing) is found to be lacking when compared to the attention that homosexual prohibition receives. There is a huge homeless problem in America. Does it make sense to picket and blame American churches for the problem? No. As Christians, our battle should be the same one that Jesus fought.

Another early Christian document that mentions Arsenokoites is a narrative called the Acts of John. It is understood that the person who is the subject in the 'Acts of John' is the same John who authored the last book of the Bible, the 'Revelation of Jesus Christ'. In the Acts of John, John is visiting Ephesus where he performed healings and preached the Word of God. The translator of this passage, M.R. James, is best known for his work as Provost at King's College, Cambridge, UK in the early 1900s, his translation of the New Testament Apocrypha and the numerous ghost stories that he wrote. In the following thirty-sixth section of the Acts of John, we find that James translated *Arsenokoites* into the English word,

Sodomite. Sodomite is an interesting word itself, in that it is not used anywhere in the Old Testament to describe the people of Sodom. Basic logic would suggest that people from Sodom would be Sodomites, like people from Moab are Moabites. However, the only Old Testament usage of sodomite is in its description of a male temple prostitute. Additionally, the use of this word in the Acts of John translation reveals the eisegetical bias of Bible translators of the past.[84] These translators superimposed the definition of a male prostitute onto the men of Sodom, thus their name would forever be associated with prostitution. If the Bible scholars were correct in this translation of the Hebrew word *Qadesh*, than is not the sin of Sodom *prostitution* and not homosexuality? Homosexuality and prostitution are not the same, so Qadesh cannot mean both homosexual and male prostitute.

Acts of John, Section 36

"Thou that rejoicest in gold and delightest thyself with ivory and jewels, when night falleth, canst thou behold what thou lovest? thou that art vanquished by *soft raiment*, and then leavest life, will those things profit thee in the place whither thou goest? And let the murderer know that the condign punishment is laid up for him twofold after his departure hence. Likewise also thou poisoner, sorcerer, robber, defrauder, *sodomite*, thief, and as many as are of that band, ye shall come at last, as your works do lead you, unto unquenchable fire, and utter darkness, and the pit of punishment, and eternal threatenings. Wherefore, ye men of Ephesus, turn yourselves, knowing this also, that kings, rulers, tyrants, boasters, and they that have conquered in wars, stripped of all things when they depart hence, do suffer pain, lodged in eternal misery."[85] [Italics mine.]

Here we find both Greek words, Malakos (<u>soft raiment</u>) and Arsenokoites (<u>Sodomites</u>) being used within the Acts of John passage. Neither word is translated as homosexual. In biblical scripture, the word Sodomite means a male prostitute. Although there is no sexual context in this section of the Acts of John, the preceding section has a similar sexual theme as the First Corinthians 6 passage of the Bible. Without a sexual context, why would a homosexual reference appear in the middle of this passage? It has no context here. Arsenokoites, more than likely, is mistranslated to mean a male prostitute. In sections 34-35, John talks about the arrogance the Ephesians exhibited as it related to their physical appearance and wealth. It seemed the Ephesians were using their bodies for some type of gain (promise) which John said would end in the grave. John referenced how their adultery, which is linked to idolatry, would also bring them to an end. His description of the Ephesian people is very similar to the description of the Corinthians; wrathful, drunkards, quarrelers who are enslaved to shameful and dirty desires. Read his description below:

Acts of John, Section 35

"Thou also that art puffed up because of the shapeliness of thy body, and art of an high look, shalt see the end of the promise thereof in the grave; and thou that rejoicest in adultery, know that both law and nature avenge it upon thee, and before these, conscience; and thou, adulteress, that art an adversary of the law, knowest not whither thou shalt come in the end. And thou that sharest not with the needy, but hast monies laid up, when thou departest out of this body and hast need of some mercy when thou burnest in fire, shalt have none to pity thee; and thou the wrathful and passionate, know that thy conversation is like the brute beasts; and thou, drunkard and quarreller, learn that thou losest thy senses by being enslaved to a shameful and dirty desire." [86]

The sins mentioned here are similar to the Corinthians passage, but do not provide a definitive argument that Arsenokoites refers to homosexuality. Arsenokoites does not appear in Section 35. Section 35 of the Acts of John discusses sexual sin. This is the appropriate place to discuss arsenokoites, if it is indeed a sin of a sexual nature verses a sin of social injustice. It is interesting to note that the word Malakos also appears in section 36 with Arsenokoites, just as the two appear together in First Corinthians 6. Also, notice that Malakos shares the same *clothing context* in Matthew 11:7-8 and *clothing definition* in First Corinthians 6:9, not a sexual context. The bottom line is we *know* that Malakos does not have an intrinsic sexual connotation and we do not have a definite knowledge of the meaning of Arsenokoites. The meaning of Arsenokoites has a sexual connotation, typically used in an exploitive context but it is not used in a homosexual context outside of the Bible.

Malakos

The Greek word Malakos in verse 9 of First Corinthians is translated in English to mean 'soft'. The word only appears two other times in the New Testament and specifically refers to soft clothing. It also has been translated as a negative metaphor in the following concepts: effeminate, catamite (younger participant in a homosexual encounter with an adult male), male prostitute (sexual orientation not specified), or a boy kept for homosexual relations with a man.[87] Within the Corinthian passage, the term cannot be used to refer to a male prostitute as Paul already used the term pornos, which means a male prostitute or fornicator. Malakos is a term that has been used derogatorily since ancient times. However, to get a clear understanding of why Paul used it, we need to revisit the context in which First Corinthians was written. You will notice a connection between the locations of Ephesus, Rome and Corinth, and the subject of 'homosexuality' in Paul's writings. As mentioned previously, Paul was living in Corinth when he wrote to the church at Rome. He was living in Ephesus when he wrote to the Corinthian church. He had the same cultural and societal influences when he wrote to these two churches. These same influences would have impacted Apostle John, the subject of the Acts of John mentioned earlier.

In Corinth as well as the larger surrounding area of Greece, pagan worship, prostitution and pederasty were a part of the culture. These vices were not acceptable to the growing Christian community and Paul addresses them in his letter to the Corinthians. St. Clement offers some information about the social climate that continued beyond Paul's time.

> "St. Clement of Rome is believed to have been the fourth bishop of Rome and served during the last decade of the first century. Around 96 AD, he sent a letter from the Church of Rome to the Church of Corinth, a major city in northeastern Greece and the site of St. Paul's evangelization. This letter, known as Clement's *First Epistle to the Corinthians*, is most likely directed against *immoral practices of prostitution connected with the Temple of Aphrodite*. In the letter, Clement expresses his dissatisfaction with events taking place in the Corinthian Church and asks the people to repent for their unchristian ways."[88] [Italics mine]

The practice of temple prostitution that Clement referred to was still occurring at least 50 years after Paul wrote to the Corinthian Church. It is noted that this prostitution was in connection with the temple of Aphrodite. Tradition shows that this temple employed more than 1,000 female and male prostitutes with whom its 'worshippers' could have sex. Greek tradition has engrained within it, the acceptance of prostitution and other sexual immoral practices that were considered a 'normal' part of society, but unnatural to the Corinthian believers. Its existence and practice was hundreds of years old by the time Paul wrote to Corinth. The sexual customs of the Greeks had existed for hundreds of years before Paul wrote to the Romans and Corinthians. However, prostitution was not the only immoral practice.

There was a statesman, lawmaker, and lyric poet known as Solon, who lived in Athens, Greece during the 6th century BC.

> "[This] legendary lawmaker is credited with having created state brothels with regulated prices. Prostitution involved both sexes differently; women of all ages and young men were prostitutes, for a predominantly male clientele. Prostitution was a part of daily life in ancient Greece, and the more important cities, and particularly the many ports, employed a significant proportion of the population and represented one of the top levels of economic activity. It was far from being clandestine; cities did not condemn brothels, and they existed in plain view."[89]

It is known and accepted in society that young men served as prostitutes for male clients. Additionally, pederasty was another Greek tradition where a formal bond between an adult man and an adolescent boy was established outside the boys' immediate family, consisting of loving and often sexual relations.[90] It has been said that

Solon instituted this tradition within the society of Athens. He was also known for composing poetry praising the love of boys.[91]

> "A number of laws addressed the issue of relations between men and boys. None but citizens could engage free boys in pederastic relationships *('A slave shall not be the lover of a free boy nor follow after him, or else he shall receive fifty blows of the public lash.').* In Athens the practice of pederasty was more freely constructed than the more formal Cretan and Spartan types. Men courted boys at the gymnasia or at the baths and on the streets of the city. Fathers wanting to protect their sons from unwanted advances provided them with a slave guard, titled 'pedagogos', to escort the boy in his travels. The courtship often was fiery, involving street fights with other suitors, sleeping on the threshold of the beloved as a show of sincerity, and composing and reciting love poems."[92]

Paul's awareness of the history and practices within the Greco-Roman society provided him with the backdrop for his writings to the Corinthians.

Malakos is not a term that necessarily denotes homosexuality. In and of itself, the word does not have a sexual meaning or connotation. There are some possible uses of the word during the 1st century. It may have been a derogatory euphemism, akin to 'faggot' in 21st century vernacular to describe a homosexual. It may have been used to describe an effeminate man. Effeminacy in men is not a guarantee of same sex attraction or homosexual behavior; it is a description of demeanor or disposition. Some heterosexual men also may be described as effeminate. A lack of bravery was considered to be effeminate in ancient Rome. Why did Paul use Malakos in First Corinthians 6:9? It is unclear. It is highly probable that the term was a euphemism used to give a physical description of the *feeling* of the adolescent boys' body. The culture of the day had women of all ages as prostitutes. However, only young men and boys served as prostitutes and participants in pederastic relationships. Solon referred to the 'deflowering' of young boys in the same manner as young girls. Deflowering is the 'taking away' of innocence or virginity. Flowers have the connotation of being soft and delicate. Malakos could have been the description of the physical softness of a youth in a pederastic relationship, as opposed to the harder, more developed body of an adult man.

Malakos can be found in two other New Testament scriptures: Matthew 11:8 and Luke 7:24. Both of these passages are concerning John the Baptist. Their context can shed some light.

Matthew 11:7-8

"As they departed, Jesus began to say to the multitudes concerning John: What did you go out into the wilderness to see? A reed shaken by the wind? But what did you go out to see? A man clothed in *soft* garments? Indeed, those who wear *soft* clothing are in kings' houses." [Italics mine]

The word for *soft* in this verse is <u>Malakos</u>. It is referring to soft or fine clothing that royalty would wear as opposed to the more coarse type of garments John the Baptist wore. Malakos is not being defined in any sexual context in the Matthew passage, including a homosexual one. The only way the word could have meant something different than soft clothing in the First Corinthians passage would require it to be used euphemistically. A euphemistic use leaves too much speculation as to the true meaning, since more than one type of illegal sexual activity occurred in Corinth. Some scholars have said that the words Arsenokoites and Malakos used together define a homosexual relationship. The Arsenokoites would be the active (or penetrating) partner in the relationship and the Malakos would be the passive (or penetrated) partner. By the way, all male homosexual behavior and/or relationships do not involve penetrative activities. The Malakos would be the softer, more feminine partner, thus a euphemism meaning the 'soft one'. Again, there is no proof that the words can be defined this way.

Paul must have had a purpose for his usage of these particular terms. If we look at chapters 5 and 6, we notice that Paul was writing to the Corinthians about the *type* of people in their city. He listed some of their behaviors. They practiced idolatry, prostitution and pederasty. In a pederastic relationship, a young boy would be the one who was penetrated. He would be referred to as the soft one, the feminine one. Paul would have been warning the Corinthians about this pagan practice, not homosexuality. The word homosexuality did not exist in the Greek language. Paul used these two words to describe the activity in First Corinthians 6. In Romans 1, he used phrases to describe the activity between two *arsen* (males) versus two *aner* (adult men). Pederasty was not solely practiced by homosexual men. Many of these men were heterosexual or at least had wives.

Pederasty was elevated to the level of an institution that was widely practiced in Greek and Roman society. In pederastic relationship, men seduced boys into this behavior with various gifts. They used their power and influence as adult males over them and the boys looked up to these men.

Arsenokoites and Malakos, at best, were used in a euphemistic context; however, their actual definitions are still not conclusive. Why do I say this? We find that Arsenokoites and Malakos are used together in section 36 of the Acts of John, however in a non-sexual context. The context of the passage is about kings and rulers similar to the Matthew 11:9 passage, which referenced soft clothing. This similarity in the two passages **cannot** simply be ironic. Let's talk another look at the Acts of John.

Acts of John, Section 36

"Thou that rejoicest in gold and delightest thyself with ivory and jewels, when night falleth, canst thou behold what thou lovest? thou that art vanquished by *soft raiment[malakos]*, and then leavest life, will those things profit thee in the place whither thou goest? And let the murderer know that the condign punishment is laid up for him twofold after his departure hence. Likewise also thou poisoner, sorcerer, robber, defrauder, *sodomite[arsenokoites]*, thief, and as many as are of that band, ye shall come at last, as your works do lead you, unto unquenchable fire, and utter darkness, and the pit of punishment, and eternal threatenings. Wherefore, ye men of Ephesus, turn yourselves, knowing this also, that *kings*, rulers, tyrants, boasters, and they that have conquered in wars, stripped of all things when they depart hence, do suffer pain, lodged in eternal misery."[93] [Italics mine]

What commonality could all three terms (kings, malakos and arsenokoites) have in this passage? The connection is unclear in the manner that the words are being translated. A relationship between kings and soft raiment (clothing) is made in this section of the Acts of John. The author of this section points out *the lack of importance that precious things (fine clothes, jewelry) have when compared to one's overall life.*

He explains when a person dies; the gold, jewels and fine clothes do not go with him. He continues by saying when kings go to war, and when they die, they are stripped of these things. The list of people the author mentions in section 36 coincides with the list in First Corinthians: robbers, defrauders, thieves. The author of Acts of John mentions the same type of people, except he includes poisoners because John was given poison when he arrived at Ephesus, but it did not harm him.[94] The words <u>kings</u> and <u>Malakos</u> have a similar context and are mentioned together inside and outside of the Bible. The definition of Malakos is clearly fine or soft. However, the word that does not belong here is Arsenokoites, as it is translated to mean homosexual. The mention of a homosexual does not fit within the context of the section. The term must have a different meaning in the Acts of John as well. It seems slightly logical that the term may mean male prostitute, as prostitution is exploitive in nature, like robbery and fraud. The exploitive nature of Arsenokoites would be logical in the Corinthians passage as well, as the word is coupled with thieves, revilers and extortioners in that passage. However, the 'male prostitute' translation is not consistent in the Corinthian passage since a Greek term for male prostitute is already used there. When reading the First Corinthians passage from a Christian perspective, the act of pederasty is exploitive. This type of act is not a part of the overall theme of love and hospitality found within the Bible. In pederasty, the *Arsenokoites* exploits the *Malakos* by offering him a gift to obtain the sexual gratification he desires. The term Arsenokoites can be used in an exploitive manner to describe the exhibition of power and control over another. However, Arsenokoites cannot and does not define homosexuality. Pederasty is no more a definition for homosexuality than a man raping a woman defines heterosexuality. This is why the Sodom and Gomorrah account in Genesis 19 is not about homosexuality. It is a story of attempted rape. Rape is abusive and exploitive regardless of its homosexual or heterosexual nature. In evaluating the Bible passages and the historical Christian writings, the only clear and concise translation of *Arsenokoites* and *Malakos* is to describe a pederastic relationship between adult men and young boys, not homosexuality in general.

Let us take a look at the other terms to review from First Corinthians 6: Fornicators, Idolaters, and Adulterers. These terms further clarify the overall context of Paul's message to the Corinthians.

Fornicators

What is a fornicator? It is not a modern word. Typically it is only used within the context of church culture. The Greek word for Fornicators is *Pornos*. The modern day church has understood this word to identify sexually immoral people in general. Fornicator is considered a catch-all term that provides an umbrella for all other sexual sins. This is evidenced by how the word has various translations in some of the modern Bible versions as well as its usage in church vernacular. The Revised Standard Version (RSV) of the Bible translates Pornos as 'immoral'. This is a very general definition, which could encompass almost anything, if the scripture is not read in proper context. The very popular New International Version (NIV) is a contemporary English translation of the Bible published in 1978 and updated in 1983. The NIV translates the word to mean 'sexually immoral'. In some respects, the NIV version was published because the RSV did not completely follow conservative Christian teaching. The NIV has "preserved traditional Evangelical theology on many contested points for which the RSV has been criticized."[95] Interestingly, both the RSV and NIV texts have misrepresented the context and intention of the word Paul used in this verse. This error still appears after the 1983 update of the NIV. The word Pornos (Fornicator) does not simply denote general immorality or sexual immorality. Pornos is a word with specificity. A *Pornos* or fornicator is a man who prostitutes, sells or exchanges his body to another as a response to lust; a male prostitute. Etymologically, the term is rooted in selling. This clarification allows us to see Paul's intent when describing the type of people the Corinthian Christians should not associate with.[96] This specific term addressed the Corinthian residents who Paul had in mind; those who were committing pederasty and engaging in sexual activity with prostitutes at the temple of Aphrodite. For these individuals, their sexual behavior was transactional.

When reading the book of First Corinthians, we must determine the overall message Paul was trying to convey. Paul was writing a letter, not a book of the Bible. Individual verses cannot be highlighted to meet preconceived theological positions. Paul's intent was to "resolve doctrinal and practical problems within the *local* church".[97] [Italics mine] The local church was specifically the Corinthian church. The specific problems Paul addressed were idolatry, male and female prostitution and pederasty, all in conjunction with the pagan worship at Aphrodite's temple. Once these truths are understood, then relevant applications can be made to our contemporary culture and setting.

Fornication

The word fornication is not found in First Corinthians 6:9-10. It appears a few verses later. However, I need to clarify the meaning of this term. It is assumed that the sexual act of <u>fornicators</u> is called fornication. This is correct. However, all fornication is **not** committed by fornicators. The Greek word for fornication is *porneia*. Where pornos is used to describe sexual acts for trade, porneia has two uses. The first is to define the activity of a fornicator, which I define above. The second use is a metaphorical definition for *idolatry*. I raise this issue because Apostle Paul used both pornos and porneia in his letter to the Corinthians. It makes sense that he did, since his subject matter is idolatry and the related 'sexual' worship of Aphrodite. In First Corinthians 6:13-18, Paul starts the conversation in verse 13 by saying that 'the body is not for fornication'. He ends it in verse 18 by saying to 'flee fornication'. The word fornication in these two verses is traditionally understood to mean illegal sexual activity. However, the information between the two verses sheds light on Paul's intent. He prohibits taking one's body and joining it with a prostitute (at Aphrodite's temple) because the two become one in spirit. This would be the ultimate act of idolatry. In this verse, idolatry is *porneia*, the word translated fornication. Fornication also means idolatry with an emphasis on how illegal sexual activity can pull a person away from the true worship of God. This was the case with King Solomon in the Old Testament. Although illegal sex was the vehicle to be avoided, Paul's overall goal was to stop idolatry.

Idolaters

This word is clear and concise as it describes the cultural climate of Corinth and the surrounding areas. The Greek word for Idolators is *eidololatres,* which means a worshipper of false gods. It also is identification for anyone, even Christians, who participate, in any way, the worship of pagan deities. In First Corinthians we understand that God was establishing His church through the Apostle Paul. Verse 11 of chapter 6 says that the Lord Jesus and the Spirit of God *sanctified* the Corinthian believers. Sanctified simply means to separate or set apart from someone or something else. God was separating the spiritual beliefs and practices of His people from the beliefs of those who lived among them. This separation meant Christians could not worship with pagans in pagan temples or in a pagan manner or worship pagan deities. Paul specifically identified idolaters so there would be no ambiguity in understanding the next group he identifies.

Adulterers

Adulterers is another word which readers of the Bible take at face value. The English translation of a word does not necessarily carry the same meaning in biblical scripture as in the original Greek. Close biblical study is necessary to prevent these doctrinal misunderstandings. Paul was trying to correct this misunderstanding in the Corinthian church. The Greek word for Adulterers is *moichos.*

Moichos is a word that must be defined by its context. In reading this passage, we assume that an adulterer is a person that 'cheats' on his or her spouse. The word adulterer or adultery, in the Old Testament and New Testament, has always been connected to idolatry. The word first appears in Exodus 20:14. It is a part of the Old Testament law. "You shall not commit adultery." The Hebrew word, *na'aph* means to be with *another's* wife <u>or</u> idolatrous worship. Since Paul was so adamant about connecting these words, what do idolatry and adultery have in common? The commonality is commitment. An adulterer is one who breaks commitment or agreement with their spouse. When a man took a wife in the Old Testament, he created a covenant with her. He committed to take care of her and certain laws prohibited him from just discarding her or walking away from the relationship. The nation of Israel was also in a covenant with Jehovah, the Lord God. For an Israelite to worship another god (a pagan god), he would be breaking covenant or agreement with his true God. This is why scripture says that God is <u>married</u> to the backslider – the one who walks away.[98] Jehovah God committed to take care of Israel, but they kept walking away to other gods. Jeremiah 3:8 gives an example of the Israelites committing *adultery* against God.

> "Then I saw that for all the causes for which backsliding Israel had committed adultery, I had put her away and given her a certificate of divorce; yet her treacherous sister Judah did not fear, but went and played the harlot also."

God compares Israel's idolatry to a marriage relationship. Israel was unfaithful to God like spouses can be unfaithful to each other. Contemporary Christians can be just as unfaithful.

<u>Luke 18:10-14</u>

"Two men went up to the temple to pray, one a Pharisee and the other a tax collector. The Pharisee stood and prayed thus with himself, 'God, I thank You that I am not like other men--extortioners, unjust, adulterers, or even as this tax collector. I fast twice a week; I give tithes of all that I possess.' And the tax collector, standing afar off, would not so much as raise his eyes to heaven, but beat his breast, saying, 'God, be merciful to me a sinner!' I tell you, this man went down to his house justified rather than the other; for everyone who exalts himself will be humbled, and he who humbles himself will be exalted.

Adultery has the connotation of idolatry because at its base level, commitment is broken. This is seen in the New Testament as well. In the Luke passage above, we read about a Pharisee and a tax collector who went to temple to pray. The Pharisee thanks God that he is not like extortioners, adulterers, the unjust or tax collectors. This is a list of people who were socially and economically unjust. Tax collectors were in this list because they were dishonest in Jesus' day. They were not above extortion or 'tipping the scales' to cheat people out of their money. So, how does an adulterer fit into this prayer, since marriage, relationships, or sex is not a part of the context of this passage? The Pharisee continues in his prayer saying that he fasts twice a week and gives tithes of all he possesses. The Pharisee is trying to prove something by his statement. He is trying to prove that he is not dishonest with his money. He is not an unjust extortioner like tax collectors. He uses his money for good. *Why does he mention that he fasts twice a week?* He is trying to show his commitment to God. He is trying to prove that he is not like an *adulterer.* In the context of this passage, an adulterer (moichos) is one who is ungodly or unfaithful to God. This is the same word for adultery in First Corinthians 6:9. Adultery has a slightly different meaning depending on the context in which it is used. When adultery is mentioned in James 4:4, the context of the verse is also <u>commitment</u> to God, not sexual commitment to a spouse.

> "Adulterers and adulteresses! Do you not know that friendship with the world is enmity with God? Whoever therefore wants to be a friend of the world makes himself an enemy of God."

Sex is not mentioned in the entire fourth chapter of the book of James. Moichos (adultery) has been improperly and excessively translated to have a sexual connotation instead of an idolatrous one. In the First Corinthians 6 passage, Paul is using adultery in a sexual and idolatrous context. Idolatry refers to specific pagan practices, but in a sexual context. Adultery refers to the condition of a person's heart when being unfaithful or idolatrous. Paul was making a connection between idolatry and adultery. He warns the Corinthians not to have fellowship with people who are unfaithful and uncommitted. Why? King Solomon married unfaithful and uncommitted women. He ignored God's warning and they led him away from his God.

To summarize the First Corinthians 6 passage, Paul identifies a group of people in verse 9 and a different group in verse 10. Verse 9 describes men who are giving themselves over to idolatry and breaking their commitment to God and their own wives through Corinthian pagan practices. He does not want the Corinthian believers to engage in their wickedness. Verse 10 describes the type of men who cannot be trusted in Corinth: thieves, drunks and extortioners. Paul encourages the Corinthian believers to have their matters handled within their own Christian community. First Corinthians 6:9-10 condemns the specific homosexual related behaviors of pederasty and temple prostitution, as they relate to idolatry. However, the passage does not address nor condemn committed homosexual relationships or homosexual orientation as found in modern day society.

First Timothy 1:9-10

"... that the law is not made for a righteous person, but for the lawless and insubordinate, for the ungodly and for sinners, for the unholy and profane, for murderers of fathers and murderers of mothers, for manslayers, for fornicators, for sodomites, for kidnappers, for liars, for perjurers, and if there is any other thing that is contrary to sound doctrine."

In this book, Paul is writing to a young minister named Timothy. He gives him instruction on various issues, such as church doctrine, choosing leaders, and dealing with false teachers. Paul states that the Old Testament law is not for the righteous (Christian believers), but the lawless. He then gives a list of the type of unbelievers to whom he is referring. In verse 10, he mentions fornicators (*pornos*), sodomites (a possible incorrect translation for *Arsenokoites*, as a sodomite has historically been known as a male prostitute), and kidnappers (*andrapodistes*). We have looked at the term pornos (fornicators) in the previous section. This leaves us with arsenokoites and andrapodistes. Here is another example of where traditional teaching incorrectly opposes homosexuality. Is this translation correct using the word *sodomite*? Is the passage referring to homosexuality or prostitution? If a sodomite was a male prostitute, how did the word *sodomy,* in current vernacular, become synonymous with homosexuality, oral sex and other sexual activities between two consenting adults? Sodomy should be associated with *male* prostitution, not homosexuality. It is apparent that social opinion has made a strong influence on how this term is defined. For many years in the United States, certain states had *sodomy* laws outlawing homosexual sexual activity. Many decades ago, incorrect Bible translation made its way into the court system, creating laws based on terms that were originally misunderstood. The meaning of Arsenokoites is misconstrued, just like it is in First Corinthians chapter 6.

In the Timothy passage, an additional sin of kidnapping *(andrapodistes)* is mentioned. The term actually means 'manstealer or slave trader'. It is the idea of a slave being stolen from one person and sold to another. Here the term is coupled with Arsenokoites. The true meaning of Arsenokoites is still unclear. In Corinthians, Arsenokoites is used with Malakos to describe pederasty, an exploitive relationship between a man and a male youth. In the Acts of John, both of these words are used in a context of exploitation. Here in First Timothy, Paul is describing the men of Ephesus in an exploitive manner as well. Actually, every sin in this list is of an exploitive nature. This passage coincides with the Acts of John, as that text was also written about the Ephesians. Paul's intent in the Timothy passage was to explain the purpose of the Old Testament law. He says the law was created for ungodly, abusive and exploitive people. Could a homosexual act be exploitive? Yes, just like heterosexual acts can be exploitive. Are all homosexual acts and homosexual people exploitive? No. Paul's letter to Timothy does not condemn homosexuality; nor does he appear to be discussing homosexuality. The letter condemns exploitation. More than likely, he was referring to pederasty by mentioning the aggressor in that type of relationship; just like a manstealer would be an aggressor. I believe Bible translators are wrong on their interpretation of this passage. Again, if they were correct in their word translations, the passage does not address homosexuality.

Colossians 3:5

> "Mortify therefore your members which are upon the earth; fornication, uncleanness, inordinate affection, evil concupiscence, and covetousness, which is idolatry." (King James Version)

The word *Pathos* or Inordinate Affection has been used to indirectly refer to homosexuality. However, Pathos is the same Greek word used in Romans 1 that means passionate deeds, which is actually linked to idolatry. This verse in Colossians clearly links all of the deeds mentioned to idolatry.

2 Peter 2:6-8

> "...and turning the cities of Sodom and Gomorrah into ashes, condemned them to destruction, making them an example to those who afterward would live ungodly; and delivered righteous Lot, who was oppressed by the filthy conduct of the wicked (for that righteous man, dwelling among them, tormented his righteous soul from day to day by seeing and

hearing their lawless deeds)"

This passage makes a reference to the Genesis 19 account of Sodom and Gomorrah. This passage makes no reference to nor confirms homosexuality in the original Genesis passage. However, Ezekiel 16:49 provides a clear definition of the sin of Sodom.

Jude 7

"…as Sodom and Gomorrah, and the cities around them in a similar manner to these, having given themselves over to sexual immorality and gone after strange flesh, are set forth as an example, suffering the vengeance of eternal fire."

Jude 7 refers to the activities that occurred in the devastated cities of Sodom and Gomorrah. In the chapter on *Old Testament Homosexuality*, I covered the fact that these cities were destroyed due to their abusive lack of hospitality. Inhospitality is not just an act of being mean. It is also the practice of humiliation and abusive treatment. One of the great commandments from ancient Hebrew law that still stands today is that you "treat your neighbor as yourself." In the New King James version, this verse says that the residents of Sodom did two things: "gave themselves over to sexual immorality and were going after strange flesh". One Greek word comprises the phrase, 'having given themselves over to sexual immorality'. It is *ekporneuo*. According to the Greek lexicon, the word has the connotation of 'to go a whoring'. Its implication is not one of homosexuality, per se. In the Old Testament, the phrase "go a whoring" was related to idolatry. God did not want Israel to 'go a whoring' after idol gods.

Some readers' understanding of this phrase "going after strange flesh" to mean engaging in homosexual activity. The Greek word for strange actually translates 'other', thus 'going after *other* flesh. The complete phrase "going after strange flesh" is translated from the following Greek words: *aperchomai opiso heteros sarx*. I will define each term.

1. *Aperchomai* means 'to go away' or 'to depart'. <u>To go away</u> has the connotation of "good things being taken away from someone." <u>Depart</u> has the connotation of "going away to follow someone else." This verb phrase describes taking something good away from someone or someone departing from a path to follow someone else.

2. *Opiso* means 'after' or 'behind'.

3. *Heteros* means 'the other' or 'another'; usually it is in reference to a number (i.e. 1 of 2) or to distinguish another kind of *something*. The use of this word occurs when numbering or comparing two things. In Jude 7, there is no comparison or numbering of items occurring, so the word is being used to make a distinction. The verse uses the word "*another* flesh" without comparing the word to anything else. This same word is used in Luke 9:59, 9:61 & 14:19. In each of these verses, the word 'another' refers to *someone* else. If the Greek word *Heteros* in the Jude passage meant 'the other', the subject of <u>flesh </u>would have been referring to women, thus it would have been incorrectly used as Lot's

visitors were male. In Jude 7, the word is used to refer to another person.

4. *Sarx* means body; a living creature (man); flesh (earthly natures of man).

Given the definitions of these Greek terms, the phrase *aperchomai opiso heteros sarx* is better translated "going after (someone else's) another's body (with the intent to take something good away, as denoted in the usage of the verb, Aperchomai). This clearer translation follows the context of the breach in hospitality that occurred in Sodom. The men of Sodom tried to rape and take from Lot's visitors their respect and innocence. Again, this account of attempted homosexual rape is not the same as homosexual orientation or homosexuality. Rape of any type is a violent and unwelcome act. A person's innocence and respect are stolen. The Jude passage is not a condemnation of homosexuality. It is a condemnation of sexual immorality in general, which was *one* of the sins of Sodom and Gomorrah as well as humiliation, degradation and attempted rape.

Summary

These highlighted passages found within the New Testament concur with the overall words and ministry of Jesus the Christ. A central goal of Jesus' ministry was to tear down religious traditions that were masking themselves as true worship.

> "This people honors Me with their lips, but their heart is far from Me, and in vain they worship Me, *teaching as doctrines the commandments of men.*" [99]

Jesus' words capture the true essence of the problems found within the Greek and Roman culture, as well as the error within contemporary society's response to these scriptural passages. Paul and the other New Testament writers were addressing pagan idolatrous practices that were infiltrating the growing Christian church. Many of them were exploitive; a direct contradiction to the greatest commandment of 'loving God and loving your neighbor as yourself'. Jesus and Paul were equally against idolatry. Paul wanted to drive this point home. He used three distinct terms that all have a link to, or is used metaphorically for idolatry. They are porneia (fornication), eidololatres (idolaters) and moichos (adulterer). This current prevailing doctrine about homosexuality is equivalent to 'teaching a commandment of men'. We have discovered that male prostitution, temple prostitution and pederasty existed from at least 6 B.C. through 96 A.D. These are the activities that Paul discussed in Romans, First Corinthians and First Timothy. These passages do not condemn homosexuality or homosexual relationships or orientation. By superimposing a preconceived 'homosexual' context upon these passages, we prevent select others from truly learning about and worshipping God. The issue is not homosexuality. It is a non-essential to a relationship with God. The important issue is the worship of our Heavenly Father. Idolatry is what inhibits true worship. God is Spirit, and those who worship Him must worship Him in spirit and truth.[100]

This is what He seeks.

CHAPTER 11
Divorce

For years, I was afraid to get a divorce. Divorce is not at the top of the "things to do before you die" list. Especially for the evangelical Christian. However, my marriage had experienced ups and downs over the years and the passion between my wife and I was just not there anymore. There were many reasons that kept me in the relationship. A major one is that I did not want my children to be products of a broken home. I grew up around and am related to too many "baby daddies". I did not want to join that club. However, I could not see that my anger and suppressed sexuality, from which my anger was partly originating, had already brought tension in the home thick enough to dull any sharp knife. Not to mention the anger and frustration my wife was suffering from, as a result of her husband no longer being attracted to her. There was also the pressure of not wanting to be embarrassed. Sadly, I indeed made choices that brought embarrassment for my family and my church. We were leaders in our church. People looked up to me and my wife because of the odds we faced in our marriage. Many people knew of my 'previous' homosexual lifestyle ('He's the guy that used to be gay, huh?') and thought it was courageous for both of us to press forward in maintaining a 'successful' marriage. Things looked great from the outside, and in some respects, our marriage was better than a lot of other marriages. However, around the 10 year mark, we were both miserable. My wife was unaware of my secrets. We continued to stick it out and make it work, because we didn't want to let the church down, let our family down or ourselves down. Then there was the silent vow I made to myself. It was almost done unconsciously even before I was married. There were many failed relationships in my family and I didn't want to be counted among them. My grandmother was divorced; my aunt had been divorced three times; my sister has three ex-husbands and I believe a former fiancé. My brother could never sustain a decent relationship with a woman. He finally got married at around 40 years old. So far he is still married, some 7 years later. The good news is my closest cousin has been married for 22 years. I am proud of her for 'hanging tough' with her husband.

The couple to whom I gave the least amount of marital credit, however, were my own parents. They were never 'legally' married. As a kid, I would ask my mother for her wedding anniversary date, but she could never 'remember'. I thought it was strange, but didn't question it. She and my father wore wedding bands. We all had the same last name. They had to be married. Well, years later, my mother explained to me that they had a 'common law' marriage. No wedding ceremony. No license. She simply took my father's name, bore his children and we were a family. Period. As an arrogant Christian adult, I didn't equate their relationship to that of a real marriage. How sad on my now divorced *part! My parents met and became a couple around 1953. My father left his girlfriend and 'hooked' up with my mother. My father had recently fathered a baby girl with this previous woman. My parents stayed together until my father's death in 1989. If my math is correct, they remained committed to each other for 36 years! I was 23 years old at that time. 'Til death do you part.*

Although divorce has become commonplace in society today, historically it has been taboo in the church. Churches now have ministries for the divorced and remarried. I never thought I would be a part of that group. Well, here I am. I am not lamenting. As painful as it was, my marriage would not have gotten much better. How could it? Outside of my infidelity, it was possible *that we could have remained married. There was just one problem: my wife is heterosexual and I am homosexual. I have spent 20 years trying to be heterosexual, attempting to fulfill an incorrect interpretation of the Bible. It has also taken years for me to discover that I didn't love myself. I truly thought I did. I have worked on myself through Bible study, prayer meetings, accountability partners, support groups and psychotherapy. I have gained a lot and grown a great deal in various areas. However, there was a part of me that I did not love which was my sexuality. Most Christians would say homosexuality is a part of my sin nature, so I should not accept it. However, behavior and orientation are not the same. A thief does not have an orientation towards stealing. He may have a mental illness (kleptomania) or she cannot afford to buy the things she wants, so she steals them. The very existence of my sexual orientation was completely opposite of what I believed. This conflict in my soul has caused me to not love and to hurt myself. In turn, I have not loved my family in the way they deserve. That has all changed. I have accepted who and what I am. I have a freedom and a love for myself that I have never felt before. I am able to love my family and other people in ways that I have not before. I am able to receive God's unconditional love for me which pours out to other people. For this I am truly grateful.*

My ex-wife also needs love. She deserves to be with a man who cannot only love and cherish her (which I tried and in some ways did), but make her feel desirable and sexy, which I could not. I, in turn, did not want to lie about my feelings towards men anymore. I lied to myself and I lied to others. The only result from the lies was more and more pain. Now there are no more lies. I am a gay man and I, too, want a relationship where affection, romance, commitment and emotional connection feels genuine and not contrived. I desire to experience that kind of love as well. I believe my ex-wife and I are on the right path to reach these goals. More than a year has passed since our separation. Thank God we both can say we have experienced the 'best' divorce possible. Not to say there were not challenges, as there have been many…and difficulties continue to arise. However, we are very amicable and have each others' best interest at heart. I do not recommend divorce for every couple where one spouse realizes he or she is homosexual. Every marital and family situation is unique and decisions must be made that will best benefit that family unit. However, if divorce is inevitable, I hope the love of Christ will be displayed by each spouse to the other, even in the midst of indescribable pain. Gratefully, Christ will not allow us to handle more than we are able. For some of us, this will include carrying the enormous burden of divorce.

CHAPTER 12
On the DL (Down Low)

The term 'Down Low' has various meanings depending on who is using it. The media has made the usage of the word popular based on J.L. King's book, *On the Down Low: A Journey into the Lives of 'Straight' Black Men Who Sleep with Men*. Although the term 'Down Low' can simply mean *to use discretion*, recently it has been used to identify, stigmatize and criminalize *black* men who sleep with other men. A media frenzy has been created around the term, which has black women (or women who sleep with black men) skeptical and running scared. Keith Boykin suggests in his book, *Beyond the Down Low: Sex, Lies and Denial in Black America* that the media has defined individuals on the Down Low as:

1. Black
2. Male
3. HIV-positive
4. in relationships with women
5. secretly having sex with men

There is a subliminal racist message that can be derived from the perception that black men are the only ones on the "Down Low". There are white men (and men of other ethnicities) who are HIV positive and do not disclose, who secretly sleep with men while having sexual relationships with women. There are men of every ethnicity who are HIV negative, secretly or openly having sex with other men. Every person on the DL or is bisexual is **not** HIV-positive. Boykin continues the conversation in his book, asking the question, 'What is the Down Low'? He then gives various scenarios of people who are same sex attracted, HIV negative who practice safe sex, openly gay or closeted, some whose opposite sex partners are aware of their sexual activity with the same gender and others whose partners are not aware. He shows that the behavior of those who identify as being on the Down Low is quite different from each other. Others who society would identify as being DL really are not. This is an important distinction to recognize, as black men do not hold the exclusive right or title to all things Down Low. James McGreevey, the *white* former governor of New Jersey is proof of this point.

Non-Blacks on the DL

Who would have ever thought that in the 21st century, an organization called Straight Spouse Network would exist? I do not highlight this group for any other reason than the obvious *need* for their existence. There are straight people who have, sometimes unknowingly, married homosexual or bisexual partners. Upon discovery, the heterosexual spouse may find themselves with a dilemma. Some of these spouses see their marriages as a lie. How could their partner have deceived them? Other spouses empathize with their partners and side with them in their battle for finding truth and acceptance of their sexual orientation. They feel sorry that their spouse had to suffer in silence for so many years. Whatever position the straight spouse takes, decisions need to be made. One woman who was married to a man on the Down Low initially told me, "I didn't see that [homosexuality] in him. That's not what he was to me." She told me that gay people didn't 'bother' her and that it didn't matter. I shifted the conversation to the subject of fidelity and her personal health. She then admitted, "I didn't want to know, so I never asked him." She was aware that the rumors she had heard about her husband were true. She had been getting tested for STDs throughout their relationship. She was 'heard' him having sex with another man. The relationship eventually ended in divorce.

The Straight Spouse Network's survival is based on a need that I, and other men like me, have created in the lives of our spouses, be it intentional or not. Their existence is based on the concept of DL living. For the purpose of distinction, I will define DL as people who secretly have sex with the same gender. What is so interesting about this particular network is its membership appears to be primarily white! Yes, white. This organization was founded by a white heterosexual woman whose husband came out to her. The organization's website lists biographical summaries of its board members (men and women) whose spouses lived secret double lives engaging in homosexual liaisons. None of these board members are African American. This group's work shows that DL living is not relegated to Black men. However their existence does not minimize the threat that living on the Down Low can impose on the African American community or any other ethnic community.

As quiet as it is kept, DL living is not exclusively a homosexual activity either. In the 1980s, the famous televangelist, Jimmy Swaggart was instrumental in exposing the heterosexual DL behavior of another televangelist, Jim Bakker. Rev. Bakker was involved in an extramarital affair with a woman which led to his resignation from the *PTL Club*, a ministry he was instrumental in building. However, Jimmy Swaggart's heterosexual DL behavior was also exposed when it was discovered that he was a frequenter of prostitutes. There is a phrase, "What is done in the dark will surely come to the light." It is interesting that when some people are engaged in activity that is viewed as sinful, they will cast a 'spotlight' on someone else's behavior, in an effort to keep the *exposing light* off of their own. I have been there and done that.

The concept of being on the 'Down Low', or doing it on the 'Low', or keeping it on the 'Low' is not a new concept at all. It has been a phrase used in the African American community for decades. Keeping something on the 'Low' is slang for keeping something private or confidential…just between you and me. Here is an example. *Lisa's parents are giving her a surprise birthday party. They ask me to help invite some of her friends, but they don't want Lisa to find out. I give Lisa's friend David a verbal invitation to the party. "Come to Lisa's surprise party on Friday, but keep that on the* low. *We don't want her to find out."* The term Down Low has been widely used in heterosexual context as evidenced by two R&B artists, R. Kelly and Brian McKnight. Their songs are entitled "Down Low/Nobody has to know" and "On the Down Low", respectively. Each song talks about a man having sex with another man's <u>woman</u>. Homosexuality is nowhere in the picture.

So what is living on the DL in a homosexual context? The definition varies depending on who is defining it.

> "Some fit the definition of a man married to a woman secretly having sex with other men while other definitions range to include black men who openly have sexual and intimate relationships exclusively with men but prefer to create identities separate from what they view as "a racially insensitive white gay world."[101]

Some men who are on the DL are living lives of deceit. They deceive themselves as well as those with whom they are intimately involved. Some heterosexual men have something to hide, as in the case with these two married televangelists. They were having sex with women who were not their wives and they wanted to keep that fact hidden. Homosexual men who are living under the guise of being heterosexual are trying to hide in similar fashion. They are hiding their true sexual inclinations. They are deceiving the women in their lives into believing they are heterosexual, and possibly faithful, by keeping up 'appearances' when they are actually having homosexual encounters. Some DL men understand that their sexual/romantic attractions are homosexual while others choose not to label it as such. These individuals, who are possibly in denial or have not come to terms with their sexuality, chose to say that they are not gay or homosexual. Others hold to a belief that refraining from getting involved in a 'relationship' with a man or sharing an intimacy like kissing, will keep them separated from the category of homosexual or gay. These men may be masculine in identity and may not relate to the stereotypical portrayal of the 'less than masculine' gay man. They may use phrases like "I just mess around with guys" or "I'm a man who sleeps with men" which distinguishes them from being "gay".

Being on the DL does not only describe 'straight' men who sleep with other men. There are men who are exclusively homosexual in orientation and behavior that live on the DL. These men may have just as many reasons to keep their sexuality as secret as the DL 'straight' man, like preachers or politicians. Many African American men have a negative view of homosexual men as being weak and/or feminine. This philosophical position is rooted in ancient social beliefs of "the privileged male". In societies of old, it was believed that men were simply better than women just because they were male. Women were at the bottom of any measurement within social structure. For a man to be equated with femininity or even be associated with a woman was a social stigma. This opinion was held even during Jesus' day. His disciples were concerned about, but afraid to question, why He was found talking to a woman in public.[102] Although subtle, the fear of being too closely associated with the feminine is still engrained in the male psyche. When men and sometimes women, desire to hurt a man emotionally, they will 'feminize' him. Ironically, this psychological maltreatment has been unconsciously practiced by most of society, even those who seemingly would be opposed to it.

As a black man who is a Christian and a minister, I understand the need to 'hide' one's true sexual preference in the face of possible ostracism from their community, family, church and others. I have walked in these shoes. However, any man who *enjoys* having sex with other men is, on some level, homosexual or bisexual. His sexual attraction is homosexual or bisexual, even if he does not view his orientation as such. Physical sexual attraction is not the only factor that determines a person's sexual orientation. There is an emotional and psychosocial connectedness that two same sex people share. A refusal to verbalize these facts does not change their validity and reality. A person may believe they are bisexual; however there are very few *true,* middle spectrum bisexual individuals. By this, I mean people who are equally attracted to both genders. For many years I believed that I was bisexual. I have always found women to be attractive and even have favorite parts of their physique. My admiration of their bodies however, has not altered my attraction towards men. At a time, I was able to be sexually aroused by women and engage in sexual activity with them. (I am biologically a father.) However, this required some mental gymnastics on my part. In the latter years of a twelve-year marriage, I discovered more and more that I was solely attracted to men and not women. My true sexual orientation could not have become more evident in my inability to become aroused by my ex-wife. I have learned that verbally denying my true sexual desires has only caused me, my family and loved ones, grief. I am not bisexual. My sexual preference is homosexual. My sexual orientation is not just about sexual activity. I would be homosexual if I never had sex again. I am comfortable and satisfied sharing intimacy with a man in ways that does not occur with women.

It may be hard to understand how a man can believe that he is not homosexual or bisexual when he engages in homosexual sex for pleasure. The difficulty lies within the fallacious self-concept he possesses and possibly displays. Homosexual and bisexual men have an attraction to men and heterosexual men are attracted to women. On some level, it is just that simple. Some homosexual men attempt to hide their 'true' sexuality partly due to the pressure they feel to conform to a more traditional concept of masculinity; thus a *masculine* sexuality. Some heterosexual men also feel this pressure to conform. We use terms like "man up" or "don't let him punk you" as ways to reassure our masculine identity in ourselves and each other. It is the challenge to be brave, responsible and to accept a challenge. A prevailing assumption is that homosexual men are not brave, responsible or willing to accept a challenge. Mainstream portrayal of homosexual men usually does not fit into this model. Heterosexual men often make sure they *always* appear 'masculine' and 'straight' around their heterosexual friends, even when there is no question of their sexual preference. Society has not allowed men (or men have not learned how) to accept and love who they are, the way they are without the display of masks or meeting someone else's expectation.

Many black homosexual men choose not to be defined by a label. Men who choose not to self-identify as gay or homosexual can be classified as 'men who sleep with men' (MSM). This classification makes sense as they have sex with men regardless to their self-concept. This term can be used to identify men of other ethnicities as well. Other black homosexual men choose to not be identified as 'gay' as the term is usually associated with *white* homosexual culture.

The term 'same gender loving' has been embraced by many in the African American homosexual community.

Differences

People, who actually have meaningful relationships with homosexual people, understand that we are just regular people. All homosexual men do not fit the stereotype as depicted by the character Jack on the television series, *Will and Grace*. For those who have not seen the show, this character is portrayed as a campy, 'flaming' and effeminate white gay man. All gay men are not promiscuous. All gay men do not wear their sexuality like a campaign button. I am one of them. I have no problem telling someone I am gay and do not feel the need to deny it if asked. However, I do not have a need to let the whole world know. My sexuality is a private matter and is discussed on a need-to-know basis. However, I am not ashamed of who I am. I have no desire for anyone to look at me and say "Oh, he is gay" anymore than I want them to say, "Oh, he is black". I am extremely proud to be a black man and would not have it any other way. Being black is essential to the whole of my being, but it is not the sum of my existence. Neither is my sexuality. Other homosexuals feel this way. This is why many people are unaware that they have gay colleagues, relatives and associates. I have male gay friends who are complete sport fanatics, following entire sport seasons, quoting player and team stats and declining dates on nights that their favorite teams are playing. Some of these same guys are hard-core participants in their favorite sports, playing in baseball and football leagues. On the other hand, I have straight male friends, whose lack of interest in and knowledge about sports is proven by their inability to distinguish a shot made in basketball and a touchdown scored in football. Stereotypes do not define people; they just provide fuel for negative prejudices.

Hookups

Sexual 'hookups' are what a gay man engages in when he does not want to or cannot have a romantic or committed relationship with another man. With gay male sexual encounters, a man will 'hook up' with another guy for sex. Hookups, like all sexual activity, are not exclusively homosexual. He may feel he needs to hide his sexual attractions, so he will hook up with another guy. Hookups may happen with someone he knows; a "friend with benefits" or it may be more of an anonymous encounter with someone he just met or a total stranger he 'cruised'. However, hookups happen almost as frequently in the heterosexual community. Any straight guy will tell you about his conquest to take a girl home and sleep with her the same night he met her in a club or bar. Heterosexual activity as well as homosexual activity can be simply an arrangement of sex. Hookups between homosexual men may happen more frequently because you have two men who are looking for the sexual conquest, whereas a heterosexual woman (or a lesbian) is not necessarily looking to conquer the way her male counterpart is.

I spent many years as a gay man hiding. I spent countless hours cruising (visiting known locations where gay men meet for sex) and living on the DL (Down Low). The sexual activity I was seeking was not really what I was after. I wanted a connection to others who shared my same sex orientation. Many times, I would meet a guy and not have sex. We just talked. During this time in my life, I hid my true sexual orientation from myself out of fear and guilt. I hid it from people who could shame me, like my family and Christian friends. Believing that a heterosexual relationship could quell my same sex desires and help me remain 'holy', I decided to marry. I married one of my closest friends. I truly loved her and still do, but a few years into the marriage, I was hiding again. I feared losing so much that I resorted to a life on the DL, complete with gay hookups. At times, I would establish a 'relationship' with a guy. He and I were the only ones who knew the relationship existed for fear of exposure.

I have learned that hookups can be driven by desperation, which can lead to dangerous situations. I experienced such a hookup late one night. I was cruising in an adult bookstore during my days of bachelorhood. As the pattern goes, I made eye contact with a guy I was interested in (or vice versa, I don't recall) and we stepped outside to talk. He fit the bill for me: Handsome, muscular with an engaging smile. After we made small talk, we decided to sit in my car for further conversation. It didn't take long for my radar to detect something was strange about this individual. His conversation shifted from mild banter to his personal medical problems, hatred for the world, his desire to hurt someone, coupled with how desperately he wanted to take me home with him. He moved in closer and held my arm. My concern for personal safety was rising to an extremely high level, as his grip became tighter. I remember sensing death. I had never been in a situation like it before or since.

My initial reaction was to bolt from the car to protect myself. The problem was we were in *my* car and I would have felt stupid standing outside of my own car trying to get this guy out. If I called the police, how would I explain where I met this man, why he was in my car, and what our initial plans were? Plus I had not actually been threatened. I begin to pray and make promises to God that deep down inside I knew I wouldn't keep. "Lord, if you get me out of this situation, I will never do this again!" Well, God is merciful and gracious. He knew the emptiness of my promise, but nonetheless intervened. I began to empathize with this guy's pain over his medical condition. As I talked, his grip loosed and his demeanor changed. I tried to remain confident as I 'talked this guy down'. I didn't know that I possessed such strategic negotiation skills. After a half hour or so, I was able to convince this guy that I wanted to be his friend and that we could meet the next day to talk some more. Actually the spirit of God intervened and changed this guy's motive. I gave him the dummy home phone number that I would use. There were no cell phones in those days. It was an old disconnected phone number. I never forgot it, so it was easy to recall in case someone tried to call my bluff. The exchange was made and he was out of my car and out of my existence. I quickly drove away to a spot where I could regain my composure, thank God for His mercy and apologize for my conduct. Even though I was scared out of my mind, this encounter did not prevent me from meeting strangers in the future. Since I did not want to 'taint' my Christian image, I continued to have clandestine meetings with men.

The encounter was not my first run-in with some type of danger. A few years before, I met a guy in a different situation. I was young and very naïve. I had heard if you drove down certain streets at night with your lights off, it was a sign of wanting to hook up with someone. I never had the nerve to do this, but driving home one night I noticed another car with its lights turning on and off behind me. I thought it was strange because this was a major street and it couldn't have been what I thought. I didn't pay it much attention. I pulled over at a gas station to fill up for school the next morning. I paid for the gas and exited the convenience store. As I filled my tank, I noticed that the empty car in the other island looked familiar. It couldn't be, I thought. I returned to the convenience store to retrieve my change. I overheard the clerk and a customer talking about the college at which the customer taught. The clerks' son was a student there. The customer exited. I retrieved my change and followed suit. When I returned to my car, the other customer spoke to me and waved. I allowed his winning smile to grab my attention and we began a conversation. After some small talk, he asked if I knew he was trying to get my attention while we were driving. He confirmed my previous thought. He asked if he could call me sometime. I told him I would take his number, which I did and left.

DeAngelo and I begin to hook up whenever I was in town. I was attending school in Orange County, about 40 miles east of my parents' Los Angeles neighborhood and I lived on campus. DeAngelo was a nice guy. He wanted more from me than I was able to give him at the time, so our relationship could only go so far.

DeAngelo was patient and giving. He understood that I was relatively new at hooking up with guys. Months went by. I would call DeAngelo when I was in the city or he will call and invite me over. One evening I decided to surprise DeAngelo and dropped by his house. His car was in the driveway, so I knocked on the door. There was no answer. I thought I knew DeAngelo fairly well. It was rare that he would leave home without his car. He liked to be in control of the time when he would come and go, so he didn't like to ride with other people. I left. I visited family and friends and decided to drop by his house again later before returning to Orange County. I did so with the same lack of response. A few days later I called DeAngelo to see where he was and his brother answered his phone. "I'm sorry to tell you, DeAngelo passed away." I was shocked. DeAngelo was only a few years older than me and I was twenty four at the time. I didn't know how DeAngelo died and he didn't seem to be sick the last time I saw him. I didn't want to ask for information on the funeral. I didn't know any of his family and our relationship was basically a sexual one. I would have felt strange attending a service for him. DeAngelo and I had many things in common, one of which was our Christian faith. I knew that he attended church with an old friend of mine from high school. A few months later, I ran into my old classmate and asked about DeAngelo. He informed me that DeAngelo was found murdered in his bed! The information gathered from the investigation and interviews suggested that he might have brought someone home that he didn't know who killed him. There were no signs of struggle at the crime scene. Upon learning this, I was overcome with grief and shock.

Then it dawned on me that the day I was knocking on his door, it was very possible that he was lying dead inside!

I once asked DeAngelo if he felt safe meeting guys the way that he did (I wasn't really hooking up much at this point) and he told me that he had such a hard time meeting guys because he had to hide his sexuality from his students, family and church. Instead of coming out as a gay man, he chose to live his life on the DL. Sadly, his choices and his hiding cut his life short and the world lost out on an otherwise really nice man. I am grateful that I no longer have to live in the shadows of DL living. Hopefully, others can find strength and support to come out of the shadows as well.

I, personally, am not proud of my life on the DL. For me, DL living was about lying and deceit. Lying creates pain and regret. I wish I could say I was brave enough to finally face my reality and uncover my secret life. I was not. Instead, I was caught and exposed. As painful as it was to all of us involved, I am grateful for the exposure. It has lead to my liberation as a person and the possibility of my healing. After years of personal turmoil, my coming out has begun and I finally am able to handle who I am as a gay Christian man.

Why are some men afraid to disclose their sexual preference and no longer live lives on the DL? There are homosexual men, just like heterosexual men, who are just looking for sex. They don't want a relationship. They seek gratification and that is all they want. Some men do not want to be labeled as gay or homosexual because of social, cultural or professional reasons. Society still makes it difficult to be open about your sexual orientation. Being open does not mean you are an aggressive promoter of your sexuality, wearing buttons or displaying rainbow stickers on your car. It simply means your sexuality is a part of your person that does not need to be denied or hidden. If you are asked, you *may* answer in the affirmative about having a homosexual orientation. It is not required for anyone to disclose or discuss their sexuality, heterosexual or homosexual. However, the option is there if desired.

Labeling and discrimination are other reasons for DL discretion. When people are labeled, it allows others to put them into certain categories or 'boxes' and define them based on a label of *their* choosing. All homosexuals are not the same nor are we all comfortable being a part of one of the gay subcultures, which includes clubs, bars and partying. This is another stereotype. Some gay people enjoy the variety of mainstream living and are open about their sexuality within it.

I wrote this book because theological teaching and spiritual beliefs (specifically within Christianity) make a large contribution to why men live on the DL. Traditionally, homosexuals have been the step-children within the Christian church. On the surface, homosexuality is taught as wrong and sinful, however, many homosexuals play key roles within the church community and are secretly accepted. I have personally watched ministers teach on the 'wickedness' of homosexuality and later call their favorite (ah, em) *gay* soloists to the microphone to sing before they preach. Faith, scripture and sexuality need to be reconciled as well as an ending of marginalization and hypocrisy within the church. I have made this reconciliation for myself. Once the Bible is studied in its proper context as it relates to homosexuality, its message becomes very clear. The Bible does not condemn homosexuality. Homosexual orientation is not even mentioned. It is now time for our Christian leaders to stop the condemnation, in order to free the parishioners to do the same. The Bible teaches us that God gave Christian leaders to the body of Christ as a gift.

> "He handed out gifts of apostle, prophet, evangelist, and pastor-teacher to train Christ's followers in skilled servant work, working within Christ's body, the church, until we're all moving rhythmically and easily with each other, efficient and graceful in response to God's Son, fully mature adults…God wants us to grow up, to know the whole truth and tell it in love…"[103]

I encourage every person who is living on the DL to own your behavior, identity, orientation and sexuality. Living in secrecy and lies, not only hurts others, but it hurts you as well. Lying and deceit is not a part of the plan that God would have for your life. Lying is what is sinful, not being homosexual. However, if through lying, your DL life is sinful, what does that say about people, systems and social structures that encourage, on some level, deceitful behavior? I pose an equal challenge to political and spiritual leaders to help bring an end to the social stigmatization that homosexual people experience. Within the church community, pastors are required to search and study the scriptures to understand and teach what the Bible means, not just what it reads. Once the truth about homosexuality is understood, there will no longer be a need for living lies, as a safe space will exist for truthful living.

CHAPTER 13
What did Jesus say about Homosexuality?

There is so much controversy about what Jesus did or did not say about homosexuality. One side of this debate states that He said nothing, so His silence proves a lack of condemnation towards homosexuality. The other side references Jesus' quote of Genesis 2:24 about a man leaving his parents and 'clinging' to his wife. To them, this statement means that heterosexuality is the only valid expression of a relationship and/or sexuality. What I find is Jesus was not as dogmatic as we are about various issues or even sins. We don't see Jesus 'going off' about someone committing adultery. It would serve us well to take Jesus' position. More times than not, He would calmly 'hear a person out', state the truth and extend salvation. No picketing, no protests, no arguments. He just loved people in their current conditions and situations. This is our true responsibility as well. We are to love people, share God's Word and allow the Holy Spirit to reveal truth to them and change their hearts as He sees fit.

As recorded in the Bible, Jesus did not comment on homosexuality. We cannot say His silence is either approval or condemnation of the subject. Since there is an absence of commentary, we have to look at the things that Jesus said to determine how society and the church should treat homosexuals. Additionally, we need to see if Jesus made any inferences to homosexuality. Finally, if scripture defines homosexuality as fitting under some other broad category, did Jesus make any comments about that category?

The words that Jesus said (or did not say) are not the end-all of His message. Jesus' message was one of love for fellow man and the love and worship of God the Father. Jesus' words and message were not those of exclusion. So why is it that we, His followers, put up so many roadblocks to people coming to Him? Homosexuals are the only group that many Christians require to change before they are allowed in the fellowship. If you are open about your sexuality, you are shunned. However, if you are closeted, you are accepted with open arms… "you know, but just keep the gay thing on the low". This is a kind of 'don't ask, don't tell' policy for the church. For years, many conservative Christians have watched musicians and choir directors lead 'worship', knowing they are homosexual. There are closeted preachers who ridicule 'sissies' and 'fags' from the pulpit, only to later retreat to their own DL or other immoral behavior. Most people just turn a blind eye. Jesus does not want us to turn from anyone. He wants to love them through other Christians. In order to do so, we need to understand Jesus and His message more clearly. He is the only one who decides who can and cannot come to Him for salvation and fellowship in His church. However, some of us have a 'messiah complex' and feel we have the right to decide.

An Argument from Silence

Many Bible scholars do not believe the absence of Jesus' comments about homosexuality are important or intentional. They would say an *argument from silence* is an invalid one. I disagree. I believe Jesus' silence on the matter was both important and intentional. These scholars will mention that there are many things from which we should abstain that Jesus did not mention, like bestiality or child molestation. Bestiality and molestation cannot be linked to homosexuality because they are not homosexual acts. They are immoral sexual acts, irrespective of sexual orientation, just like rape.

In Matthew 15:19, Jesus talks about the things that defile the body. (It is assumed that Paul states homosexuality is a defilement of the body in Romans 1, but he did not.[104]) Jesus says the things that come out of the heart defile the body. He lists them to be *evil thoughts* (or bad reasoning), *murder, adultery* (sex outside of a committed relationship/marriage) and *fornication* (unlawful, idolatrous sexual activity, like prostitution). Some of these same activities are listed in Proverbs 6:16 – 19 as abominations. As we have read, homosexuality is described as an abomination in Leviticus 18:22. The Matthew 15 passage would have been a prime opportunity for Jesus to discuss homosexuality if it were the abominable or detestable activity that modern society makes it out to be. Homosexuality was not important for Him to discuss here because it was not an issue for Him. If it were, this is where He would have mentioned it. Homosexuality, definitely, is not an issue that precludes a person from salvation, which was the basis of Jesus' ministry. In light of the limited amount of times where homosexuality is 'alluded to' in scripture, it is not an issue *at all*. [105]

When you read the Bible in its broader context, you will discover that the issue of Jesus' silence about homosexuality is not an *argument from silence* at all. The teachings of Paul are based on the teachings and ministry of Jesus. Paul was imitating and continuing the preaching of the Gospel message. Both men taught against the practice of idolatry; each in the forms in which the practice presented itself in their day. The practice of pederasty and temple prostitution did not exist in the geographical areas in which Jesus ministered, thus He had no need to address these practices. However, Paul addressed them and on various occasions and locations. Why? Jesus and Paul had different audiences. Living in a Greco-Roman society, Paul preached to Jews and Gentiles, in an effort to reconcile the two groups into one universal church. Jesus' audience was the "lost sheep of Israel".[106] He focused on breaking down the religious barriers that were established and guarded by the Jewish leaders. Each man ministered to the needs and issues of the people around them. It made no sense for Jesus to preach about temple prostitution where it did not exist as it was not a Jewish practice. However, adultery and heterosexual prostitution existed among those to whom He ministered. Thus, He addressed these issues in Matthew 15:19. He also addressed adultery when He forgave the sinner woman.[107] He dealt with prostitution when He told the prostitute to go in the way of salvation in John 7:50.[108]

Love

Scripture records that Jesus kept company with tax collectors and prostitutes, which were despised by many. One of the women (some speculate it was Mary) who anointed Jesus' feet was a prostitute (a sinner). Jesus allowed her to **touch** Him. This was unheard of. It is obvious that Jesus did not condone the act of prostitution; however, he did not shun prostitutes. Did her encounter with Jesus mean that she stopped engaging in prostitution immediately? Scripture does not say. Prostitution is not a practice that a person engages in out of pleasure. It is usually driven by some survival-based need. Additionally, the human psyche has to make major adjustments in order to give such an intimate part of one self away in that manner. In this example, Jesus seems to be more concerned with the condition of her heart than her outward behavior. His concern with us is the same. Jesus' example of love should be the basis of how we treat others. No one should be marginalized or rejected in the body of Christ. Jesus never did this. Neither should we.

Jesus spoke of and displayed love often. He identified loving God as the greatest commandment to keep. He said the second greatest commandment is to "love your neighbor as yourself".[109] This is a large demographic. A neighbor is "any other man [person] irrespective of nation or religion with whom we live or whom we chance to meet."[110] Jesus says we are to love them and treat them in the same manner we would treat ourselves. This command follows the Old Testament principle of hospitality. We should consider others before ourselves. Jesus said this principle is the basis of the entire Old Testament Law.[111] As it relates to homosexuality, too many 'Christians' grossly ignore this commandment. Most often, our love has been reserved and only extended if the homosexual person wants to change her orientation, if it is extended at all. Unfortunately, society at large follows the example of Christians, however at times they take it to a level of hatred. One surprising example of hatred came from a "Christian preacher", Jimmy Swaggart. I put Christian preacher in quotes because the hate spewed by Mr. Swaggart is completely contrary to the Bible and the teachings of Jesus. During a sermon, he said,

> "I never seen a man that I wanted to marry. If one ever looks at me like that, I'ma kill 'em and tell God he died."[112]

Even if Mr. Swaggart disagrees with homosexuality, how is he representing the Christian message with such a hateful threat; not to mention that he would intentionally lie to his own God? I know his statement was probably a bit exaggerated; however, the intention of his heart was real and conveyed. The majority of the Christian community does not share in Mr. Swaggart's extreme views, but it is unfortunate that miseducated preachers are leading and teaching congregations with this type of hatred and rhetoric. He says the Bible calls homosexuality an "abom'nation" (The incorrect pronunciation is his). Not only was the word mispronounced, I am not sure if he understood its true definition. I am unaware of any formal Bible or seminary training that Mr. Swaggart has received. Nevertheless, he still serves as a pastor over a large ministry. Messages like Mr. Swaggarts' would cause anyone to question Christian love.

Affection

Jesus was a man who was secure in His identity. He was not afraid to share His love and to display affection for others publicly. I point this out because some of us men, who have been raised in the West (North America), have a 'hang up' about touching and being affectionate with other men. It is really a sad condition as God created us with a need for touch and all touch is not sensual. Some men will allow themselves to be touched under certain circumstances. Football players are not afraid to 'slap' each other's butts or 'chest bump' together on national television, but to hug or hold a man close is too feminine. It is illogical. All touch is not sexual. The act of touching can be loving, supportive and affirmative. Jesus said,

> "A new commandment I give to you, that you love one another. [In the same way] I have loved you, [in that way] you also love one another."

Jesus demonstrated this in His relationship with the Apostle John. John is known as the disciple who lay on Jesus' chest.[113] John is mentioned three times as the disciple whom Jesus loved.[114] How many men would be willing to be called the man who "Eric" loved? Not many, but Jesus and John knew who they were as men.

Some people may negatively infer that Jesus was 'soft'. He was far from being soft. Jesus is the same man who went into the temple and turned over the money tables. I will put this account into a current context. It would be like a group of men whose job was to provide monetary change to others, like at a laundry mat or grocery store. The problem was that the men were cheating everybody that came for change and no one noticed. Jesus walks in. He knows the men are cheating people, and He flips the table over. Not only does He spill all the money on the floor (where anyone could grab it), all of the money gets mixed up, so the 'businessmen' don't know what money belongs to whom. It would take a man with guts to do something like that. Jesus was very confident in His manhood and was not afraid to confront or display His love and affection to anyone. Neither was He afraid to correct social injustice. We should learn from His example.

<u>Eunuchs</u>

Although scripture does not record any of Jesus' commentary on homosexuals, He did speak about a group of people in a different sexual situation. He spoke about men who were called eunuchs. A eunuch in the New Testament (Greek: *eunouchos*) was one who oversaw the harem of various royals and monarchs. These men were 'made' eunuchs by castration in order to prevent sexual activity with the young maidens in the harem. Eunuchs were also castrated by men for other reasons. In the Old Testament, the Hebrew word for eunuch is *cariyc*, which means an official of the court. These men were also in charge of the care of the wives and concubines of a king; therefore some were castrated, preventing sexual activity. Sometimes the word was used as a general reference to a man who was castrated. It was used to describe other men who were born with an incapacity for sexual activity or the fathering of children. Were men who were not able to father children restricted from having relationships and/or marriage? In Deuteronomy 23:1 of the Old Testament Law, eunuchs were not allowed into the temple. Within Deuteronomy, this command follows various commands related to the stoning of adulterers and precedes a command that disallowed 'bastards' from entering the temple. A bastard would have been a child born illegitimately, of mixed heritage or of incest. If this restriction existed today, most of a church's membership would not be allowed to enter the sanctuary. Again, these Old Testament restrictions do not apply to our contemporary times and culture.

Jesus spoke of eunuchs in Matthew 19. He described three types of eunuchs: those who were born with the inability to father children / engage in sexual activity; those who were made eunuchs by men; and those who choose to be eunuchs for the kingdom sake. The first group's condition is clear. The second was a group of men who were castrated. The last was a group of men who decided to not marry or bear children for the kingdom of God. Jesus went on to say that whoever could accept this condition of being a eunuch should do so. He was referring to those who *chose* to be eunuchs, as the other two groups had no control over being eunuchs. In Jesus' statement, He was giving men a choice of a lifestyle of a eunuch. His statement clarified that being a eunuch for the kingdom was not a requirement.

Why do I mention eunuchs in reference to homosexuality? It is widely believed that Genesis 2:24 establishes that all valid relationships are only in the context of a marriage between one man and one woman. It is also believed that Genesis 1:28 is a command for *all* mankind to procreate and populate the earth. The history of Israelite men throughout the Old Testament invalidates a 'command' that all relationships were to be between one man and one woman, as polygamy was a way of life and not condemned by God. Polygamy served a purpose in populating the earth during that time in history as well as being a part of the socio-economic culture of the day. Large families were equated with wealth. The need to populate the earth no longer exists and in modern society. There is no need to have multiple wives to create large families and clans. Therefore, Genesis 2:24 cannot be used to mandate that all relationships exist only between one man and one woman. Genesis 1:28 cannot be used to demand that all people procreate. When Jesus quoted Genesis 2:24, He did not condemn, correct or comment on the historic behavior of polygamy. We do not find God condemning any polygamous relationship in the Old Testament. Jesus did not establish marriage as being between one man and one woman in His statement in Matthew. He simply stated what the conditions surrounding a divorce were to be and He addressed how women were to be treated as it relates to a divorce. Once He made this statement, He immediately begin to talk about how some eunuchs were born without the ability to have sex or father children and those who choose not to have sex or father children. In the face of Genesis 1:28, if eunuchs were given a choice to procreate or not, how is Genesis 2:24 a command preventing relationships between one man and multiple women or two men or two women? In His commentary about eunuchs, Jesus would have contradicted scripture if Genesis 1:28 were a command for all people to fulfill.

Let us take a look at marriage. In scripture, a marriage became binding once it was consummated. Basically, if the couple did not consummate their marriage, it was not legitimized. In the contemporary church, it seems the preference is for a homosexual person to marry the opposite gender (if they do not wish to remain celibate), in order to have the semblance of a good and obedient Christian. Some homosexual people have the ability to engage in heterosexual sexual activity. Other homosexuals cannot fathom the idea, just like many heterosexuals cannot imagine engaging in homosexual sexual activity. Sexual ability is not solely based on mechanics and equipment. Desire is usually required for consummation to occur. If a certain homosexual is unable to perform heterosexually, how can they consummate a marriage with an opposite sex person? If a homosexual participates in a wedding ceremony, says vows at the altar, and signs a marriage license, does that make them married in the eyes of God? Or is this 'marriage' a lie? The people who witnessed this ceremony may be fooled but God knows the truth. What about the heterosexual eunuch? (For sake of discussion, a modern day eunuch would be a man born intersex or deformed.) This man is attracted to the opposite sex but is unable to perform sexually. Can he consummate a marriage and is it legitimate in God's sight, if he cannot? Marriage is not a formula that can be reduced to one single passage in scripture. Marriage cannot be solely relegated to an activity. We must determine God's intention and purposes for marriage and how it affects the people involved.

<u>Sodom and Gomorrah</u>

The Sodom and Gomorrah story is one of the most popular biblical accounts quoted in reference to the 'sinfulness' of homosexuality. This account is also the most misunderstood and incorrectly interpreted passage of all the references to homosexuality. The Apostles Matthew, Mark and Luke, all captured a version of Jesus' message to seventy of His disciples that He sent out for ministry. In this passage, Jesus made a reference to the city of Sodom. One of the things Jesus was teaching these missionary disciples was sole dependence on God. In Luke 9:58, Jesus explained to them that He had no home of His own. He also had to trust God alone for food and a roof over His head. Jesus wanted the disciples to follow Him and trust God in the same manner. In the New Living Translation of Matthew 10:10, Jesus gave instruction for the missionary journey by saying,

> "Don't take any money with you. Don't carry a traveler's bag with an extra coat and sandals or even a walking stick. Don't hesitate to accept *hospitality*, because those who work deserve to be fed." [Italics mine]

Jesus understood that hospitality was an important custom of His day, just like in the days of Sodom and Gomorrah. These disciples were traveling from town to town, sharing Jesus' message. As they traveled, they needed places to stay and food to eat. Jesus knew that some households would welcome the disciples, feed and care for them, free of cost. However, Jesus also knew that there were households that would not adhere to the custom of hospitality. So He told His disciples,

"Now whatever city or town you enter, inquire who in it is *worthy*, and stay there till you go out."[115] [Italics mine]

In the original Greek language, a *worthy* family would be one that was congruous or exhibits harmony towards travelers. Basically, the worthy family would be a safe and appropriate place for them to lodge. Once they found a worthy house, they were to greet it and speak a blessing of peace over it. By greeting the house, they would be testing the head of household to see if they would receive in return the proper greeting, which normally would be a kiss and an embrace, welcoming them to stay for a while.[116] Jesus' instructions continued,

> "And remain in the same house, eating and drinking such things as they give, for the laborer is worthy of his wages. Do not go from house to house."[117]

If the host city did not receive Jesus' messengers and their message, the messengers were to "shake the dust off of their feet" and proclaim "the Kingdom of God has come near you" as an indication that the people who rejected them were "heathens" and "defiled". Because these hosts withheld their hospitality from the messengers, Jesus pronounced,

> "…it will be more tolerable in [the judgment] Day for Sodom than for that city."

Here is the million dollar question that no one seems to ask. Why would Jesus compare these cities to Sodom if Sodom was punished for their involvement in homosexuality? In this passage, there is no reference to homosexuality. There is no seemingly logical connection between the disciples' journey and Sodom. However, there is a reference to hospitality in these gospel accounts. We also learned in the chapter on *Old Testament Homosexuality* that the *true* sin of Sodom was their abuse of and violence towards their visitors and overall disregard for hospitality. Therefore, it makes sense that Jesus would compare these cities to Sodom. Not only does it make sense, but **Jesus' very words validate that the sin of Sodom was about hospitality and not homosexuality**.

In the *Old Testament Homosexuality* chapter, we also discovered that a parallel incident occurred among the children of Israel in Judges 19 – 20. In this account, a fellow traveling Israelite (called a Levite) attempted to find lodging within a community of his distant relatives. This group repeated the same abusive and inhospitable behavior found among the Sodomites by rejecting one of their own Hebrew brothers. As a result, they sexually abused and murdered one of his companions. Prior to giving the seventy disciples instructions in Mark chapter six, Jesus reminded the disciples that,

> "A prophet is honored everywhere except in his own hometown and among his relatives and his own family."

Neither was the Levite in the Judges passage. Jesus' experience with his own people parallels the Levites' experience in Judges 19.

Jesus had plenty of opportunity to condemn homosexuality. He did not. In the Gospel accounts of Matthew, Mark and Luke,

Jesus himself referenced the same story that modern Christians and society in general, reference: Sodom and Gomorrah. Throughout the ages, homosexuality has been attributed to these people as their sin and cause for the destruction of their cities. The words *sodomy* and *sodomite* have been coined to reference homosexual acts. It is interesting that the head of the Christian church himself, Jesus Christ, did not mention, reference or remotely allude to homosexuality when he spoke of Sodom and Gomorrah as recorded in these three gospel accounts. He knew and taught the correct context of the Sodom and Gomorrah story from Genesis 19; how to treat visitors, neighbors, sojourners and those who are different from you with respect and hospitality. The people of Sodom did not do this. This was their sin. **At least that is what Jesus said.**

Summary

As far as homosexuality is concerned, there is no record that Jesus made any condemning statements. However, what He did say validates why the reasoning behind the current prohibition of homosexuality is faulty. Homosexuals, like heterosexuals, are not required to procreate; therefore, homosexual sex is not prohibited due to the inability of same sex conception. Jesus' quote in Matthew 19 demonstrates that He was most concerned about how women were being treated in their relationships. Women were marginalized and the abuses inflicted on them were easy, frequent and acceptable in society. His reference to male and female in the beginning was validating the creation of families and for them to remain intact versus divorcing women and leaving them destitute.

The words and character of Jesus do not support the rejection of and ill treatment towards homosexual people. Jesus gave us an example (without reason) of a people (eunuchs) whose sexuality was not the norm (heterosexuality). He did not condemn them for the difference of their sexual orientation. He did not condemn homosexuals either. Neither should we.

CHAPTER 14
Orange Breasted Girl

It wasn't out of the ordinary that I was home alone on a Saturday. My own teenaged children have served as babysitters for my younger children. I would have thought my mom would have made my brother babysit. Not this time. I sat in a green velvet armchair underneath the black velvet painting of the woman with a single teardrop rolling down her cheek. The melancholy sounds of Bill Withers' "Ain't No Sunshine When She's Gone" played in the background of my mind. Or maybe my mother left the record player on. I don't remember. Bill always spoke the feelings from deep in my heart. At the time, my parents' marriage experienced so many ups and downs; I often wondered who was the one crying in the picture. The picture may have served my mother well, as a constant reminder of her sadness. Depressed as usual, I sat staring into space, wishing I was someone else. Mommy always kept the drapes closed and the windows shut. It was the stuffy and stale house of a cigarette smoker. It was dark and I let the darkness envelope me.

I wished I was happy. I wished I was a girl. I stood up and walked towards the kitchen. I pushed aside the green and gold plastic beads that served as a makeshift door, dividing the breakfast nook from the living room. It was the 1970s in all of its glory. Mommy kept a basket of fruit on the table. It was mainly for my father, the emotionally elusive and most times physically absent man in my life. The basket held oranges. Today, the oranges belonged to me. I picked up two perfectly round oranges and said to myself, "These will do." I walked back into the living room with an orange in each hand. I stood in front of the huge wall mirror that was opposite our drapery-concealed window. Our house was tiny. No matter how many mirrors we had in our living room, our house was not going to get any bigger. Nine hundred square feet is nine hundred square feet, mirror or not. I lifted my shirt and placed my fructose-filled 'breasts' underneath. No one was around to criticize or stop me. I stared at myself and slipped into a world of fantasy. I slipped into a world where I controlled the people and the people loved me for who I was. I pranced around the living room like an actress. I wanted to feel attractive and desirable, but not necessarily beautiful. In a confused way, I still wanted to truly be the handsome little boy Mommy always said I was. I never saw him in the mirror though. Today I imagined he was there and I was him -- my fantasy of confusion.

Growing up, I was not the most masculine or attractive guy in the world, but I really didn't want to be a girl either. All I wanted was attention and love. I wanted someone to appreciate me, give me a message that was opposite of the one I had always heard, "You are ugly." Well, to some, I probably was ugly. I was a very skinny kid with tight kinky hair that I hated to comb. I had severely crooked teeth from a fall I took at five years old. I was sensitive and emotional, intuitive and introspective. I was a prime target for ridicule and rejection. My world of reality was too painful to live in, so it was safer to escape to a world of fantasy. So I did just that...I admired the girl in the mirror with the orange breasts. People would love her. She had them all fooled. She had me fooled. I stared at her. I admired her until I heard my mother coming up the walkway. Fantasy aborted. Before she could get inside of the house, the orange-breasted girl was gone and my mother's compliant but confused son had returned. She greeted me with, "How's my sweet boy?"

My response was "good Mommy, I'm good".

CHAPTER 15
Gender Identity vs. Homosexual Orientation

I never really wanted to be the "Orange Breasted Girl" or any other girl. I lived in a world where sexual differences were frowned upon. Even at an age so young where I did not truly comprehend sexuality, I knew my feelings were to be kept locked inside. During this time in my life, I did not understand that I was homosexual, but I definitely perceived a lack of satisfaction in others regarding my *maleness*. For years, I believed I was a girl born in the wrong body. I would cry out to God, asking why this mistake was made. Why couldn't I be *boy*-enough? I would later understand that I **was** boy-enough. My different-ness made others uncomfortable, but nothing was intrinsically wrong with me. Sexuality is not black and white. The lack of comfort that others felt was projected onto me and I ceased being comfortable with myself. Everyone wants to be accepted for who they are. In some ways, this was not a part of my experience. I learned to create a world of fantasy where ridicule would not be a part of the landscape. It became a safe place for me to live…so I thought.

Within the subject of homosexuality and sexuality in general, there is the related but separate issue of Gender Identity. Gender identity is defined as an individual's self-conception as being male or female, as distinguished from their actual biological sex.[118] In other words, gender identity is how individuals see themselves as male or female. This definition is a little restrictive in that it is currently based around the issue of transsexualism and/or transvestism. Gender identity is defined on a continuum. It is how individuals see themselves within a range of masculine and feminine. Every sexual being has self-identification **along** this spectrum. Gender identification is **not** a static position; it is more of where the person feels they fit within the spectrum of masculinity and femininity in relation to their biological sex.

Dr. Joseph Nicolosi, a clinical psychologist, is the author of *Reparative Therapy of Male Homosexuality: A New Clinical Approach.* At the time of this writing, he specialized in treating homosexual men who are dissatisfied with their sexual orientation and/or behavior. In other words, he practices ex-gay therapy. I have read at least three of Dr. Nicolosi's books and at one point identified myself as a dissatisfied homosexual man – an ex-gay. I saw myself in the same way as one of his clients.

> "For many years I thought I was gay. I finally
> realized I was not a homosexual but a heterosexual
> man with a homosexual problem."[119]

For years, my faith in and understanding of the Bible led me to believe it was required that my sexual identity be that of a heterosexual man. After much biblical and psychological study, introspection and conversations with other homosexual men, my understanding of sexuality has, once again, broadened. I now understand myself to be a homosexual man because I have little to no sexual or psychosexual attraction towards women. Sure, I can look at a woman and determine that she is beautiful and attractive. My ex-wife is a very physically attractive women. However, it used to require a significant amount of work on my part to get aroused by the opposite sex, which sometimes required fantasizing about being with another man. This is a common thread that I have heard from countless other heterosexually married friends who are homosexually oriented. Sexual arousal with a female, obviously, was possible as I have fathered a child, but sexual attraction and natural inclination towards females is not there. On the other hand, I am naturally aroused by a man, both physically and emotionally, without any overtly sexual overtones being displayed by him. Again, sexual attraction is not solely about sex. Chemistry and connection play a significant role.

I describe myself as homosexual but I do not overtly identify myself as homosexual. I will clarify the difference. Self-description is a statement that tells or gives a representation of oneself, like "I have brown hair and brown eyes." Self-identification is how you associate or recognize yourself to be. Self-identification is the acceptance of your own values and interests within a social group. I choose to simply *identify* myself as a man. No further identification is needed. Personally, I do not need to be in the group of heterosexuals or homosexuals. Here is an example of how this difference is displayed. There are 3 women and 1 man in a room. I am instructed to find someone with the brown hair. This person may be a woman or a man or everyone in the room. If my instructions are to find a man, there is only one option. So, as far as description goes, I *describe* myself as homosexual because it is only a part of who

I am. I do not *identify* myself as a homosexual, anymore than I identified myself as a heterosexual. I am so much more than my sexual preference.

There is a misconception that all homosexual men are in one box, one category. Typically this category assumes that most homosexual men lean more towards the feminine side of the gender identity spectrum than not. This categorization can be labeled as gay. What is the difference between a gay man and a homosexual man? The difference is the term homosexual is usually related to sexual attraction, sexual arousal and sexual behavior. It is more of a clinical term. The word gay is usually related to homosexual culture, homosexual society and social behavior, thus a sociological word. Someone told me that I am not gay; I am just sexually attracted to men. Supposedly, I was told this because I do not fit into a gay stereotype or "gay culture." If this is true, there are plenty of homosexual men who are not "gay".

Gender Identity

In Dr. Nicolosi's book, *Reparative Therapy of Male Homosexuality,* he states

> "Many homosexuals are attracted to other men and their maleness because they are striving to complete their own gender identification."[120]

According to Nicolosi, these homosexual men have suffered from "male gender-identity deficit." Based on reparative therapy rules, he believes that gender identity determines sexual orientation. The more comfortable a man is with his masculine gender identity, the more heterosexual he will become. If this is true, what is the 'break-even' point between homosexuality and heterosexuality? How do we measure when a person is comfortable with their maleness? Once you reach a level of comfort, what happens if your level of attraction to the same sex does not change? Gender identity and sexual orientation are not that concrete and simplistic. Furthermore, this gender identity deficit rule does not consider men who are "masculine" in behavior who are attracted to men who are "feminine" in behavior. How are these "masculine" men trying to complete their gender identification in a man who seemingly is "less" complete? And what about two feminine men or two masculine men?

I have spent many years in therapy, researching homosexuality and applying the reparative therapy principles I have learned to my life. I can say that I have successfully 'repaired' a lot of my gender-identity issues. Every person may not feel their gender identity is damaged, however my identity was in need of repair. I am very proud to be a man and very comfortable with being masculine. I no longer put on an act, in an attempt, to appear more masculine than I am. People, who have known me for any significant amount of time, have commented on my masculine presence. However, my sexual orientation is homosexual. On a scale, I am a lot more masculine than feminine; however I possess so-called feminine attributes, like in the way I express empathy and compassion. Most people possess traits that are opposite of their biological gender. I will not say that gender identity is not related to sexual orientation, but I do not believe that it is the definitive driver of it. Furthermore, my sexual orientation does not require healing or curing. Nicolosi says,

> "Growth through reparative therapy is an ongoing process. Usually some homosexual desires will recur during periods of stress or loneliness. Rather than cure, therefore I speak of the goal of change, in which there is a shift in the identification of the self. While he may continue to have homosexual feelings, a man will usually no longer be identified with those feelings. Within that essential meaning of transformation, the client gains new ways of understanding the nature of his same-sex yearnings…Rather than focusing on the idea of cure, we should think in terms of reduction of homoerotic needs through healthy, non-erotic male relationships. Healing will range from partial, to significant, to complete freedom from unwanted homosexual attractions. For some men, heterosexual marriage will be possible."[121]

Nicolosi, like others who disagree with homosexuality, are attempting to help homosexual men with their *behaviors*. According to them, success is measured by a "reduction" of homoerotic needs being met. My *unwanted* homosexual attractions were based on a belief I developed from social and church influences. Based on reparative therapy theory, my homosexual attractions needed to be reduced, in order to fit into the 'model' of success. I have not experienced that this reduction is possible. For many years, I lied to myself in hopes that the reduction would occur. It did not. This falsehood, not only hurt me, but everyone around me. Living a lie caused me to behave in ways and engage in behavior, I never thought possible. Additionally, sexual attraction is only one component of sexual orientation. Once I was finally able to accept my sexuality, regardless of others' opinions and beliefs, I have been able to stop the pain and live in truth. My homosexual orientation is no longer unwanted. I live with a level of honesty that I never have before. I have such peace and happiness. I am no longer the angry man of denial that I once was.

Society, gay and straight, supposes that a person has to live life under a label of gay or straight. There are many homosexual men who carry themselves in a very masculine way (naturally, not by any choice), who are comfortable engaging in predominately heterosexual contexts without "wearing" their sexual orientation. This does not mean that they are hiding it. Sexual orientation does not naturally come up in every conversation, and most times it is not relevant or appropriate to discuss it. The labeling and noting of distinction comes from the individuals who are uncomfortable or fearful of homosexuals based on some bias or ignorance. These individuals need to categorize others to meet their personal needs of comfort and control. There are many heterosexuals who are comfortable being around their homosexual friends and loved ones. A homosexuals' orientation is no more the focal point than the heterosexuals'. In Dr. Nicolosi's practice, he has observed the following:

> "The fact that so many men continue to feel "dis-eased" by their homosexuality can be explained in one of two ways. Either society and the Judeo-Christian ethic have coerced these individuals into thinking they have a problem; or, the homosexual condition itself is inherently problematic."[122]

I agree with the first statement wholeheartedly. It is one of the reasons I wrote this book. I want my readers to understand homosexuality from the position of what I am terming a "non-gay" homosexual man. I am not denigrating gay culture. Every homosexual person is not comfortable or interested in it. And like most subcultures in society, gay culture contains elements that I personally find distasteful and inappropriate. We are all different. I may receive flack from gay men who will say that I am exhibiting homophobic and self-hatred behavior by my position. That is okay with me. I can only be who I am. Another reason I wrote this book is to shed light on the inaccurate interpretations of the Bible, which have caused people to feel that homosexuality is problematic. There is no inherent problem with homosexuality. Problems come with individuals. The behavior of individual homosexuals can be problematic to society, just like some heterosexual behavior.

Heterosexuality will always exist and will always be the dominate sexual orientation of people – by God's design. But all people are not heterosexual. Homosexuality holds no threat for heterosexuality. Heterosexuality is not facing extinction or some spiritual attack. However, gay couples will continue to raise healthy, well-adjusted heterosexual children, just like straight couples raise healthy, well-adjusted homosexual children. Heterosexuality and homosexuality can easily co-exist, if certain individuals will be open-minded and less fearful. People do not choose and are not influenced to "become" homosexual by seeing or being around someone who is. This is the most ludicrous fallacy that comes out of our conservative society. If this were true, we would see more 'successful' changes from homosexuality to heterosexuality. If this were true, there would be little to no homosexuals in the Christian church due to the fact that the majority of its members are heterosexual. The type of logic that says a person's sexual orientation can be changed by mere association is nonsensical.

All homosexuals are not trying to impose their "lifestyle" on the heterosexual population. Some gay activists try to make a statement with their overt "in your face" style of living, but this does not represent all homosexuals. This type of expression will always exist among groups of marginalized people. This is what the media sells to the general public. Sensationalism sells and the various forms of the media are in business to make money. The general public buys it and spreads the misinformation around. This is why mainstream local news programming is a joke. How many stories can you hear in one night about shootings and robbery? It is believed by some, that crime only occurs in one type of neighborhood, by one or two ethnic groups. The media sells this misinformation. One reason it appears that homosexuality is being "forced" upon society is because homosexuals want to be accepted for who they are. Some parts of society do not want to accept homosexuals. In recent years, homosexuals have felt safety, courage, or support in their efforts to 'come out' and live their sexual orientation openly. What many do not understand is that gender identification and sexual orientation are related, but not synonymous. There is a difference. During the final stages of my coming out process, I incorrectly reconciled my belief this way: *I was a heterosexual man with a homosexual problem.* Because I struggled with gender identity issues as a child, one of the *successes* from my reparative therapy work was my ability to fully identify as a masculine man. I always desired to possess a masculine identity; I just didn't think that I was capable of doing so. In my early years, I simply did not feel that I fit within the world of masculinity, largely because of my non-conformity to traditional masculine affinities like athletics. Once I learned to accept who I am and to enjoy the things that interest me, I was able to fully understand and embrace the masculinity that I already possessed. Masculinity is what I feel inside. Masculinity is not only the sum total of physical traits, characteristics and mannerisms. Masculinity contains within it, strength, courage, responsibility and caring. What is displayed externally is subject to an individual's own interpretation. Gender identity, like sexual attraction, is on a continuum. On one end of the continuum resides some very masculine gay men and on the other, some very effeminate straight men. A person's gender identity does not solely drive their sexual attraction. I believe there are men and women who *perform* under a gender identity that is false. They wear their feminine or masculine 'identity' as a badge of honor, an act of rebellion or as a political statement. However, their performance is not necessary. False identity will not change society; living in truth will create the change. I am relieved I can be me. I don't have to be a sports fanatic to be a man or masculine. Now that I have eliminated the pressure, I have found that I actually enjoy watching a game of football and can understand it…for the most part.

For those individuals who choose to identify more with a gender that is not traditionally associated with their biological sex, so be it. Let's not allow our fear of the unknown and the misunderstood keep us from loving and helping our fellow man.

Christians Out of the Closet

We are starting to see Christians 'come out of the closet' and acknowledge that they love God and are gay. R.J. Helton, Gospel recording artist and top finalist in the first season of the show, *American Idol* shared on a radio show in October of 2006 that "Just because I am gay does not mean I can't love God". He actually came out during the interview on the radio show. Another American Idol top finalist, Clay Aiken hit the height of controversy when he came out in September of 2008 as a gay dad, shortly after his son Parker was born. Aiken grew up and identifies as a Southern Baptist.[123] Ironically, in 2007 prior to his coming out, Aiken was scheduled to perform a Christmas concert at Central Christian Church in Wichita, Kansas. The church demanded to know if he were gay, prior to allowing him to sing. [124] Helton, on the other hand, was one of the performers during a New Year's Eve celebration at Faithful Central Bible Church a few years ago. However, this was prior to Helton's 'coming out'.

Azariah Southworth, former host of the Christian music reality TV show, The Remix, came out in April of 2008. This disclosure brought an end to his Christian television career. Ray Boltz, a long-time contemporary Christian music singer-songwriter came out in September of 2008. Interestingly, but not surprising, none of these men are African American. The only 'famous' man of African descent to come out of the closet in recent years is John Amaechi, the former NBA player; however, he does not identify himself as a Christian. Sheryl Swoopes, a WNBA basketball player is an African American woman who came out in 2005. Sheryl identifies herself as a Christian. One of her biggest concerns when she came out, was how was her mother's church friends were going to respond to her lesbianism.[125]

Then there are the untold numbers of everyday Christians who are tired of lying to themselves and others about their orientation and identity. These Christians are grappling with their faith, the biblical texts and their relationships with God and are being honest with who they really are.

Identity

I can be identified by my name, Kevin. I am the son of my parents. I am the father of my children. I am homosexual. I am African American by heritage. I am male. I am over six feet tall. All of these factors contribute to my identity. There are other characteristics that are not mentioned here. However, I feel the most important element of my identity is that I am a Christian. I can be identified by my relationship with God through Jesus Christ. He is my Savior and that is why I can identify myself as a Christian. I am a child of God. Personally, I believe this should be the most important factor in everyone's life; how they relate to God. Some people are unsure of what their relation to God is. Some people do not care. Others have experienced fractures and strains in their relationship with Him and do not know what to do about it. Still, others have not had the opportunity to have a relationship with Him yet. Wherever you may fit in this scenario, you may find the answers you seek in the next section.

CHAPTER 16

Salvation

Luke 10:25-37

And behold, a certain lawyer stood up and tested Him, saying, "Teacher, what shall I do to inherit eternal life?" He said to him, "What is written in the law? What is your reading of it?" So he answered and said, "'You shall love the Lord your God with all your heart, with all your soul, with all your strength, and with all your mind,' and 'your neighbor as yourself.'" And He said to him, "You have answered rightly; do this and you will live." But he, wanting to justify himself, said to Jesus, "And who is my neighbor?"

Then Jesus answered and said: "A certain man went down from Jerusalem to Jericho, and fell among thieves, who stripped him of his clothing, wounded him, and departed, leaving him half dead. Now by chance a certain priest came down that road. And when he saw him, he passed by on the other side. Likewise a Levite, when he arrived at the place, came and looked, and passed by on the other side. But a certain Samaritan, as he journeyed, came where he was. And when he saw him, he had compassion. So he went to him and bandaged his wounds, pouring on oil and wine; and he set him on his own animal, brought him to an inn, and took care of him. On the next day, when he departed, he took out two denarii, gave them to the innkeeper, and said to him, 'Take care of him; and whatever more you spend, when I come again, I will repay you.' So which of these three do you think was neighbor to him who fell among the thieves?"
And he said, "He who showed mercy on him." Then Jesus said to him, "Go and do likewise."

This previous passage is commonly known as the parable of the Good Samaritan. I like to refer to it as the parable of the *Arrogant Lawyer*. It is the account of a Jewish lawyer who asked Jesus how to inherit eternal life (salvation). The man who asked Jesus about eternal life was a scribe. Scribes were responsible for maintaining legal and religious traditions within the Jewish law. They were meticulous about the observation of Jewish law and were responsible for recording it. Since they were responsible for the law, they were considered lawyers of their day. In a modern context, they were more akin to a law professor. When the man approached Him, Jesus knew that he was a scribe, so He turned the question back to him. Jesus told him, 'You know the law. How do you interpret it?' (Jesus' answer also validates that every reader of scripture is also an interpreter.) His answer was to love God with everything you have and your neighbor as much as you love yourself. Jesus answered, 'You are correct. Do this and you will have eternal life'. We must pause here. <u>Jesus gave a clear answer for salvation.</u> Why as Christians do we feel we need to add to this definition? In my experience in the Christian Church, I have seen and heard people answer differently than how Jesus answered. We start off with 'you must accept Jesus as your Lord and Savior'. This is inclusive in Jesus' statement of 'loving God with your heart, soul, strength and mind', as the Father has stated that salvation is in His Son and Jesus has said if you know Him than you know His Father. However, we tend to look at a person's outward appearance and add additional requirements. If a woman consistently wears short skirts and has no regard to how it affects others, we will say she can't be 'saved'. Is this true? This woman may have an issue with propriety and needs to be taught what is decent attire and why. However, does her appearance really have anything to do with her salvation? What about the openly homosexual person? He is attracted to the same gender. Does his orientation exempt him from eternal life? Jesus never said these were preemptors, so how can we?

I know my statement is a bit of a generalization because all Christians do not believe or behave this way. However, there is some truth behind it. Many people believe that Christians are hypocrites, but not necessarily because we lack perfection. Sometimes the way we share our message gives the impression that people have to be perfect. It may not be just what we say, but how we live. We say that we have a 'relationship' with God; however, we have a laundry list of rules to follow. If you were a Christian, you wouldn't do this and this and that. Oh, but good Christians do this and that and the other. This sounds more like religion than a relationship. It is our need to adhere to religion that brings complication to a relationship with God. Most evangelical Christians will quote Apostle Paul's words from Romans chapters 3 and 6 for a definition of salvation. However, Jesus Himself made it clear and simple in Luke 10:25-37. Our contemporary Christian behavior is very similar to the Pharisees and Scribes of the New Testament. Apostle Paul said, "We have been released from the law so that we serve in the new way of the Spirit, and not the old way of the written code." It seems as Christian believers, we still prefer the old written code to the freedom of God's Holy Spirit.

As Christians we should desire to reach people who are not interested in coming through the doors of a church. However, we need to know why they are not interested in coming to a church, or why they shy away from having a conversation with a Christian. What perception do they have of Christians that is not our intention, but nonetheless is true? In the book, **unChristian**: *What a New Generation Really Thinks about Christianity…and Why It Matters*, authors David Kinnaman and Gabe Lyons reveal some "outsiders' most common reaction[s] to the faith." According to Kinnaman and Lyons, non-Christians believe "Christians no longer represent what Jesus had in mind, which Christianity in our society is not what it was meant to be". They share an interviewee's quote from their extensive research.

> "Christianity has become bloated with blind followers who would rather repeat slogans than actually feel true compassion and care. Christianity has become marketed and streamlined into a juggernaut of fearmongering that has lost its own heart."[126]

It seems that those who are looking at us Christians from the outside, see some inconsistencies in what we say versus what we do. I agree and I have been personally guilty of this error. The question is what needs to change in us, if anything and how do we make that change? The answer can be found in this passage of Luke. We cannot be like the lawyer who questioned Jesus. The lawyer asked Jesus, 'Who is my neighbor?' He was not asking Jesus for clarification. He wanted to be able to justify his behavior. He was a religious purist. He was not going to count anybody and everybody as *his* neighbor. He was hoping Jesus would give him some sort of religious 'out'. Jesus goes on to describe a story where a man was beaten, robbed and left for dead. In the story, two different Jewish religious leaders saw the beaten man and did nothing. The first priest saw him from a distance and decided to cross the street before he got too close to the man. If the priest had touched the man to determine in fact that he was dead, the priest would have been ceremoniously unclean for weeks, unable to perform his religious duties. The second priest walked over to the man, observed his condition, did nothing and walked away - maybe for the same reason. Then came a Samaritan man...

Before I continue the story, I want to explain who the Samaritans were. The Samaritans were the most despised people in the eyes of the Jewish community. The Samaritan people were proof that racism, bigotry and separatism existed during the New Testament era. Samaritans were an interracial people who were half Jewish and half Assyrian. From a religious standpoint, they believed and worshipped in a similar manner as the Jews. Due to their captivity in Assyria, they assimilated some pagan practices in their worship that did not fit Jewish law. The Jews were purists, so they did not accept the Samaritans. However, it is this 'pagan' who Jesus used as his example of salvation in action.

The way Samaritans were treated reminds me of how homosexual Christians are treated within our own churches. This Samaritan man did the exact opposite of what the religious priests did. He provided care for the wounded man. He took him off of the street and put him up in a hotel so he could recover. He paid the hotel bill and promised to pay whatever balance remained. This is radical inclusive Christianity in practice. Jesus told the lawyer, 'Go and do likewise.'

If Jesus' definition of salvation is true, why can't homosexuals be Christians if they choose to accept Jesus Christ as Savior? I am not suggesting that the tenets of the faith and scripture be altered in any way. They cannot be. Every homosexual person is not a Christian nor is interested in becoming a Christian. However, there are many who are interested in becoming Christians and many are Christians already. What the latter two groups would like is to be accepted within the body of Christ. We might ask ourselves, what is preventing them from being accepted?

Traditionally, salvation within the Christian faith is based on the personal belief that Jesus Christ is the Savior for all humanity. It is understood that every human being is born into a condition called sin, which separates the Father God from His loving creation, humanity. The way in which humanity is united to Father God is through is through the death and resurrection of Jesus Christ. Since Father God has always desired a relationship with humanity, He, through His Spirit, calls, woos, pursues, desires and draws people to Himself. The relationship starts with a person acknowledging that they are a sinner (specific sins are irrelevant), believing that Father God has provided salvation through the death and resurrection of Jesus Christ, and by accepting Jesus as his Savior, which is the gift of salvation. Once a person acknowledges their sin through prayer and accepts Jesus as their Savior, their relationship with God is established in Heaven and begins on earth. This salvation is a gift that cannot be taken away. It is eternal and lasts forever.

The most wonderful thing about this gift is it requires almost no action on the part of the receiver. Other than believing and accepting Jesus as their savior, there is no additional action needed. Although God makes changes in our lives as we come to know Him better and as He reveals Himself to us, He does not require anyone to change anything about themselves, upfront. He simply wants them to come to Him. Here is salvation presented in a mathematical equation:

Salvation = <u>Jesus Christ, mankind's savior</u> + *your acceptance of Him.*

Jesus plus your belief in Him as Savior equals salvation. That's it! Jesus is enough and all that is needed. Here is a Bible passage that illustrates this point: Romans 3:23-26

Salvation is a free gift from God that comes alive through our personal faith in Jesus Christ. We cannot add any kind of work, behavior, action or change to the gift because God wants salvation to be His gift alone. If we could start an action or stop an action to gain the gift, then it would be possible for someone to say that they were instrumental in gaining the gift somehow. God does not want us to be able to say that. Once we are in a relationship with God, He impacts our life for the better. God is in the business of making people better and actually uses 'His' people to help other people in that process. He wants each of us to join Him in this work.[127] As we begin to know God better by reading and studying His Word, the Bible, He begins to reveal to us how we can be more like His son, Jesus. We are called Christians because we are in a process of becoming like Christ. God shows us what we are to be like. He also shows us the areas of our personal lives that are not like Jesus. He provides a way for us to move from where we are to where He wants us to be. This is the work of the Holy Spirit, which happens throughout our lifetime as Christians on earth.

Since salvation is a free gift that we cannot do anything to earn or receive, there is nothing in our lives we need to change in order to receive it. This would include homosexuality. Even if a person's homosexual orientation could be changed, it would not be necessary for salvation. God wants to have a relationship with every person, homosexual, heterosexual or asexual. Sexuality is irrelevant. Receiving the love that God is extending to you is what is most important. Once this love is received, then change comes. It is a spiritual process. As we come to learn about Jesus, our spirit becomes alive and connects with His spirit and our desires begin to change. Something within us makes us want to be better people – to be more like Him. This desire for change is out of our control. If you desire to have a relationship with God, pray this simple prayer.

Dear Jesus,

I am a sinner. I believe that you have provided a way for me to have a relationship with Father God. I accept you as my Lord and Savior. Thank you for my salvation and new relationship with Father God. Amen.

It is that simple. Welcome to God's great big loving family.

CHAPTER 17
Summary: Where Do We Go From Here?

We go to God. We need to trust that God knows what He is doing and He says what He means. We need to understand that our attempt at being religious is not the same as worshipping God and serving his people. He made that clear with the parable of the Good Samaritan. When God expresses His disapproval of the way a group of people treats other people groups, we need to believe Him and not come up with our own opinion. God demonstrated His disdain for the way the residents of Sodom refused to share their town and accommodations with strangers and sojourners, yet modern day Christians conduct themselves in the same manner with homosexuals. Jesus Himself confirmed as their sin, Sodom's lack of hospitality, which was manifested as abuse and violence. He instructed His disciples on how to respond to people who would not welcome them nor offer them food and shelter during their missionary journeys. "Shake the dust off of your feet...it will be more tolerable for Sodom and Gomorrah in the Day of Judgment than that city."[128] Could Jesus have been any clearer indicating a lack of hospitality as the sin of the people of Sodom? He paralleled the experience of His disciples to that of the angelic visitors of Sodom. It seems when we do not understand why God makes the decisions that He does, our human nature will concoct a justification or reasoning. We do this so God can continue to make sense to <u>us</u> and appear just. It is our responsibility to get God 'off the hook', right? Wrong. By doing this, we fail to realize that we are leaning to our own understanding and failing to acknowledge who God is.[129] It is apparent in scripture that how we treat our fellow man (hospitality) is more important to God than our sexuality. Even when we read about adultery in the Bible, most times the focus is on the breaking of a commitment versus the sexual act itself.[130]

We need to believe God and the testimony of the scriptures. He is not bothered or threatened by homosexuality. People are. Homosexuality is a part of society that is not going away. How can it? It has been a part of human nature since the very beginning. Somewhere between two and ten percent of the world's population is homosexual. These people will not magically disappear. I certainly hope not, as I am one of them. Instead of marginalizing and discriminating against us, society needs to educate itself about homosexuality and sexual orientation as a whole. Education will empower society to embrace us as individuals and people.

My admonishment to my fellow preachers and pastors is to look at the subject of homosexuality objectively. As some of you read this, you may be cringing. God does not want our belief to be based on the beliefs of the majority nor based on the historical belief of others. In every situation, he wants our belief to be tempered with investigation. If you believe you are a Christian because someone told you that you are, then you are sadly mistaken. A reading of one verse or two does not confirm your salvation either. For every scripture that teaches salvation by faith in Jesus (Romans

10:9-10), you can find a scripture that appears to teach that salvation is based upon some effort or work of your own. (James 2:20). How do you reconcile this seemingly conflict? You do so, by holistically studying the Word of God. The same principle applies to the subject of sexuality and homosexuality, specifically. Ministers and lay Christians alike need to gain a clear understanding of sexuality, if we intend to be good and effective ministers. The ostracizing and denigrating of homosexuals must stop, if you agree with our 'presumed' lifestyle or not. I say presumed because there is no single type of lifestyle for homosexual people just like there is not a single type for heterosexuals. As children, we are taught that people are like snowflakes; no two people are exactly alike. This concept applies to all people, including homosexuals. Within the homosexual world, just like the heterosexual one, you will find people who are celibate or promiscuous, altruistic and giving or selfish and self-absorbed, family oriented and those who have no familial desire, those desirous of long term committed relationships, and those who will forever be single and 'play the field'. I will not even mention the variety within the sexual act itself. Every type of sexual act that some homosexual individuals engage in, there are heterosexuals who also indulge. Every act! With that said, we need to stop alienating homosexuals based on their 'immoral' behavior because all homosexuals do not engage in *all* behavior. Some may be surprised to know that there are homosexual people who are not only celibate, but virgins, who are waiting to find committed partners before engaging in any sexual behavior. I know some of these individuals personally and they are not even Christians! This is their personal moral choice.

Additionally, we need to remember that homosexuals have families and loved ones who are members of our congregations. Ministers must be mindful of the words they use when referring to those who are homosexual. It hurts our members when we use words of hate and condemnation towards gay people. The Apostle Paul encourages us this way:

> "Don't use foul or abusive language. Let everything you say be good and *helpful,* so that your words will be an encouragement to those who hear them."[131]

How many of us have heard a sermon where the preacher said that 'sissies', 'faggots' or 'dykes' were going to hell? Many of us. How many have heard a sermon where the preacher said an adulterer, an unwed mother or God forbid, the man who impregnated her, were all going to hell? Probably very few if at all. Neither are these individuals called derogatory names. Some of our sermonic messages are very inconsistent.

At times, the preached word requires a warning to the people who are listening. People need Jesus. As a minister, I am the first to say it. However, I believe a sermon will be better received when it shares how to obtain the awesome benefit of an abundant life with God, here on earth and beyond, versus a harsh word that simply says, if you don't watch out, you are going to hell. If the gospel message is intended to 'comply' people to come to God, this is not compelling. The gospel message does not have to be "watered down" to compel. The former method is *helpful* and *encouraging*. The latter can be a destroyer of hope in God.

Remember there is a difference between sexual orientation and sexual behavior. Understanding the difference between the two will help us understand why homosexual people are not sinners. In very simplistic terms, sexual orientation determines whom people are attracted to on a social, physical, and emotional level. Sexual behavior is the physical activity between two individuals. If homosexual <u>orientation</u> is a sin, the same measurement must be used with heterosexual <u>orientation</u>. Thus, on some level, heterosexual orientation could be subject to the categorization of sinfulness. If so, what is the measurement? The *possibility* that a homosexual <u>could</u> have sex with someone of the same gender no more makes her a sinner than the *possibility* of a heterosexual having sex with the opposite gender makes him a sinner. The *possibility* of sexual activity does not make a person sinful, just like the owner of a car who drinks alcohol, does not make him a drunk driver. He may be a drinker. He may be a driver. It does not mean he does them simultaneously. Sexual orientation is not sinful, be it homosexual or heterosexual. Orientation just... is. Some say that the Bible does not mention the creation of homosexual people. This is true; however, it does not mean that God did not create us. The Bible also does not mention the <u>creation</u> of eunuchs[132], however Jesus did acknowledge their existence by birth, so they were obviously created and they served a purpose.

So, then, what is the issue with homosexuality? Why is there such disdain for us? Why does the church condemn us more than any other people group? Is it because our sexual attraction is different from the majority of society? Is it because heterosexuals are uncomfortable with same gender attraction? As quiet as it is kept, some homosexuals are just as uncomfortable at the thought of opposite-gender sexual behavior. Their feelings, however, do not invalidate heterosexual expression.

For a group of people who have experienced a history of oppression, it does not seem logical for African American to oppress another group, overtly or covertly. As African Americans, we are still battling issues of racism in America. Is the current climate like that of the days of the Civil Rights Movement? I do not believe so; however, racism is alive and well in the hearts of many Americans and the fabric of our society. Although, on January 20, 2009, former Illinois Senator Barack Obama was elected as our first African American U.S. president, our battle against racism still continues. With this thought in mind, why do some African Americans still have contempt toward homosexuals? Homosexuals are an alienated minority group as well. Socially and politically, we are looked upon with disdain. During the AIDS crisis in the early 1980s, the Reagan Administration refused to take a serious look at the growing epidemic. His response was silence. Many of his supporters are a part of, what some call, the 'religious right'. The late Rev. Jerry Falwell is one of them, who has been quoted to say, "AIDS is not just God's punishment for homosexuals; it is God's punishment for the society that tolerates homosexuals." It is statements and beliefs like this that continue society's ill-informed opinion about and response to homosexual people. It is not ironic that Rev. Falwell was also a supporter of racial segregation during the Civil Rights Movement. It took many years for Rev. Falwell's position to begin to change. In 2005, Falwell was quoted saying that, as Americans, the LGBT community has the basic civil right to employment and civil marriage, like all Americans.

Some African Americans are put off by the comparison of the Gay Rights Movement to the Civil Rights Movement. They believe that homosexuals have chosen their lifestyle, thus they should not receive 'special' rights. I disagree. Homosexuals are people who contribute to society in every way that heterosexuals do and civil rights for homosexuals are not special rights. They are human rights. Dr. Martin Luther King, Jr. gave his famous 'I Have A Dream' speech at the 1963 March on Washington rally. This march was influential in outlawing and eliminating racial discrimination in public education, public areas and employment practices, as well as disbanding the discriminatory voting practices that kept African Americans out of the political process.[133] Dr. King's speech and dream focused on a future built on racial reconciliation. Dr. King could 'see' a time when blacks and whites would coexist as equals.

Dr. King also had a close relationship with a man that does not come up in many conversations. Dr. King had a close advisor and friend by the name of Bayard Rustin. Rustin was an African American civil rights activist who studied Gandhi's teachings of non-violence, and counseled Dr. King to dedicate himself to these same principles. Rustin served as one of Dr. King's main advisors and mentors during the Civil Rights Movement. Rustin was one of the main organizers of the 1963 March on Washington. Bayard Rustin was an openly homosexual man.[134] Mr. Rustin was openly homosexual at a time when homosexuality was <u>criminally</u> offensive. How could Dr. King **not** have been accepting of Rustin's sexual orientation? There is no public record of Dr. King verbalizing his acceptance or rejection of Rustin. However, many civil rights leaders and supporters put demands on Dr. King to distance himself from Rustin. Dr. King did not do so. What further validates Dr. King's position on homosexuality was his widow's stance for the rights of the LGBT community. The late Coretta Scott King said,

> "Homophobia is like racism and anti-Semitism and other forms of bigotry in that it seeks to dehumanize a large group of people, to deny their humanity, their dignity and personhood. This sets the stage for further repression and violence that spread all too easily to victimize the next minority group."

Mrs. King understood, very well, the message of equality that her late husband so eloquently espoused. Mrs. King publicly linked the Civil Rights Movement to the Gay Rights Movement in her statement,

> "I still hear people say that I should not be talking about the rights of lesbian and gay people. ... But I hasten to remind them that Martin Luther King Jr. said, 'Injustice anywhere is a threat to justice everywhere.' I appeal to everyone who believes in Martin Luther King Jr.'s dream, to make room at the table of brotherhood and sisterhood for lesbian and gay people."

Dr. King, Mrs. Coretta Scott King and Bayard Rustin are three prominent African Americans whose position and messages cannot be denied. They each understood that homosexuals are people who deserve love and respect from and within humanity. It is a simple right that is ours because we are just that...human.

HIV/AIDS and the Church

"Let me just put this in perspective: If HIV/AIDS were the leading cause of death of white women between the ages of 25 and 34 there would be an outraged outcry in this country." —U.S. Secretary of State and former First Lady Hillary Clinton

It is no secret that the rates of HIV infection in the Black community are at an alarming rate. Here are some recent statistics:

- African Americans make up approximately 13% of the American population, however, we account for 49% of all AIDS cases in America. [135]
- Almost half of the new HIV infections reported in America are among African Americans. [136]
- Almost half of all African American men who have contracted the HIV virus engage in sex with other men. [137]
- 75% of African American women who have contracted the HIV virus were possibly infected by having sex with men as opposed to intravenous drug use or some other method. (This statistic does not conclude that all of the men that these women had sex with were gay or bisexual men. Some of the men with whom these women had sex, may have contracted the virus from having sex with other women, intravenous drug use or some other method)

African Americans are known to be a religious people. This means that these statistics are affecting members of our churches. I have had personal friends within my local church to become infected with the HIV virus. Some of them are still with us; others have passed away. The truth about homosexuality obviously needs to be addressed, but so do HIV and AIDS. The church can help decrease these alarming numbers by engaging in the battle against AIDS. I don't want to sound like there are no churches engaged in the fight.

My former local church and other churches have held testing events as well as provided counseling and support to those who are affected by this disease. However, an overwhelming majority of the church at large just ends the conversation at abstinence. Abstinence is definitely one way to address the AIDS epidemic in this country; and it is effective with any sexual orientation. However, can we assume that abstinence is a way of life for everyone? Is our ministry only to other Christians who believe the way that we do? Most conservative churches hold the position that sex outside of marriage is a sin. I am not here to debate this point. However, churches, Christians and pastors alike, know that all of its fellow unmarried members are not practicing abstinence. There are as many children conceived and born out of wedlock within the church as outside of it. So the abstinence message is not enough. Why? Because people's lives are at risk. This does not mean that abstinence needs to stop being preached. It simply means that additional messages need to be added to the sermon.

T.D. Jakes, senior pastor of The Potter's House church in Dallas, Texas said the following in an online article for the Black AIDS Institute entitled 'We Are On The Roof Again'.

> "We do not have to agree with people on every detail to help save lives. The vision for the church was and still is to minister to hurting people -- a place where all types and descriptions could find healing and restoration for their souls... Tomorrow we can lobby, debate, and argue our theology. But while our men and women are dying seven times more rapidly than their white counterparts who are also infected, we do not have the luxury to politicize mercy nor allow our theology to defray the real mission of a state of emergency for which we find ourselves engulfed." [138]

I agree with Bishop Jakes. People are dying and on some level, we need to put the theological debate aside. Actually, we need a better understanding of each other's position in the debate. Another step that Bishop Jakes and the Potter's House have taken to address the issue of homosexuality and its connection to the church was their participation in the "American Family Outing". [139] American Family Outing is an event sponsored by Soulforce.org. Traveling during the summer of 2008, lesbian, gay, bisexual, and transgender people & their families met to create dialogue with six of America's most influential evangelical leaders & their mega-churches. Hopefully, more conversations like this will happen throughout the country to address the ill-effects resulting from misunderstanding, misplaced anger and disdain for homosexuality. Rob Woronoff is a former Program Director with the Child Welfare League of America. He has had experience working with gay youth during his professional career. He says,

> "...the power of having these conversations lies in helping people to follow a trail that begins with a misinterpretation of the Bible, which in turn supports condemnation of homosexuality, which leads directly to a sense of worthlessness among black homosexuals, which leads to high risk behaviors which result in the highest rates of HIV infection in the world. It's a road map. The science is very clear that low self-worth that results from familial and community condemnation results in the types of behaviors that lead to HIV infection. [The road map] is simply guiding people from point A (a biblically supported condemnation of homosexuals) to point B (HIV infection among homosexuals)."

This road map is helping lead many to a deadly destination. Does this excuse an individual of personal responsibility for their sexual behavior and choices? Not at all. Each of us must make choices that are healthy for us. However, it is difficult to make a healthy choice when your emotional health is not intact due to ostracism by a community that is supposed to love and accept you. A dilemma has been created because homosexuality is not a choice. It is not a choice because it is not just behavior. Sexuality is identity, orientation and behavior, be it homosexual or heterosexual.

So where does this leave us? What do we do now?

As spiritual leaders, pastors and teachers must correctly teach the Scriptures as they relate to homosexuality. This may require a reexamination of certain biblical passages for further understanding and clarification. Actually, the study and reexamination of scripture is the ongoing responsibility of every minister of the Christian gospel. I strongly encourage clergy to 'step out of the box' of the general consensus and find out what the Bible really has to **teach** about homosexuality, not just what the translators penned and what we have traditionally believed. We need to stop 'lying on God' and making homosexuality the most heinous of crimes. God, Jesus or even the Apostle Paul never said this. I do not believe that the Bible teaches that homosexuality is sinful. Scripture supports this position. The Bible does not teach that homosexuals are evil people who need to be shunned or changed, however, this is how many people, Christian and non-Christian, treat us. This opinion permeates our society, inflicting injustice upon gay and non-gay people alike.

> "In February 1996, a Pensacola, Florida judge, Joseph Tarbuck awarded primary custody of an eleven-year-old girl to her father, **a convicted murderer,** rather than to the girl's forty-six-year-old mother, a lesbian. Although the father had spent nine years in prison for killing his first wife as they argued over custody of their children, Judge Tarbuck focused on the mother: 'This child should be given the opportunity and the option to live in a non-lesbian world…the judge seems to have concluded that the mere status of being a lesbian, no matter how law-abiding, is worse than being a murderer."[140]

Stories like this prove why it is so important for society's opinion of homosexuals to be changed. The stigma of homosexuality must be removed from society. At a 2007 Democratic Primary Debate at Howard University, then Presidential candidate, Senator Barack Obama said this,

> "One of the things we've got to overcome is a stigma that still exists in our communities. We don't talk about this. We don't talk about it in the schools. Sometimes we don't talk about it in the churches. It has been an aspect of homophobia, that sometimes we don't address this issue as clearly as it needs to be." [141]

Some churches are afraid to talk about the sexuality of homosexuals because they do not want to condone what they believe to be sin. They believe that homosexual behavior is sinful and the sinfulness of homosexuality is easier to talk about. I am not too sure that solutions to the problems caused by homosexual stigmatization are easy to discuss. The truth of the matter is that people are engaging in sexual behavior, gay, straight, churched and unchurched. A broader conversation needs to be held. Bishop Noel Jones of the

City of Refuge Church in Los Angeles, California has an interesting response to dealing with "promiscuous" sexual activity.

> "The church adamantly declares that to allow the use of condoms is to condone and even to promote illicit sexual activity. Come on. What about the woman who is married to a man, and is faithful to him and he is playing around? What about the man who is married to a woman who is playing around? Use a condom on suspicion, or would you rather die with the evidence? We have to widen our scope and undo some of our traditional morals that have kept us bound. If you have a child who is running around, you have to change your attitude about whether or not to sanction the use of condoms." [142]

You do not have to condone a person's specific behavior, heterosexual or homosexual, in order to help someone…in this particular case, stay alive and healthy. We need to see the bigger picture: the bigger picture of our societal problems and the bigger picture of how the church desperately needs to be involved.

We need to follow the pattern and command of Jesus. We must love our neighbors as ourselves. We need to create an open and loving environment in our personal worlds, homes and churches for homosexual people to have an opportunity to learn about and embrace the God of the Bible. If the church community ceases the marginalization of the homosexual community, the general society will have the confidence to follow suit in accepting another part of the human race. This can only better our society. How will you do your part?

Endnotes

[1] First Timothy 2:11-12

[2] Habakkuk 2:20

[3] First Samuel 18-20 - The words that Jonathan and David shared are extremely intimate if not romantic. They loved each other as one soul. "How I weep for you, my brother Jonathan! Oh, how much I loved you! And your love for me was deep, deeper than the love of women!" These words were shared from David to Jonathan when David had to leave him.

[4] Rogers, Jesus, The Bible and Homosexuality, pg 82-83

[5] David G. Myers, Psychology, 7th ed. (New York: Worth Publishers, 2004)

[6] How to read the Bible for all its worth, Gordon and Fee, 1992

[7] Luke 10:27, NKJV

[8] Ryrie, Basic Theology, pg 114

[9] First Corinthians 7: 6, 12 & 25

[10] Fee and Stuart, "How to Read the Bible…", pg 16

[11] Ibid.

[12] The New Testament portion of the New King James Version was published in 1979.

[13] 2 Timothy 2:15; NLT

[14] The Truth about Homosexuality. 2008, January 29; John MacArthur, http://seminarian.wordpress.com/2008/02/12/the-truth-about-homosexuality/

[15] Fee & Stuart, How to Read the Bible for all its Worth, 1992, pg 136-7

[16] Read Galatians 3:21-25 for full context.

[17] John 9:3 (NKJV)

[18] 2 Samuel 12:8, NIV

[19] A pagan is a person who is not a worshipper of the Jewish or Christian God.

[20] Genesis 16:3-4

[21] Gagnon, The Bible and Homosexual Practice, pg 38

[22] © 2003 Robert A. J. Gagnon, PROF. ROBERT GAGNON'S RESPONSE TO ERIC THURMAN'S REVIEW IN REVIEW OF BIBLICAL LITERATURE Retrieved 07:35, March 25, 2008, from http://www.robgagnon.net/ReviewEricThurmanSidebar.htm

[23] Polygamy. (2008, March 22). In Wikipedia, The Free Encyclopedia. Retrieved 07:13, March 25, 2008, from http://en.wikipedia.org/w/index.php?title=Polygamy&oldid=200169014

[24] Ibid.

[25] Genesis 18:10, 14, and 19

[26] 2 Kings 23:7 states that women wove hangings for the grove in the houses of the Sodomites. They were a part of the community of Sodom.

[27] The Bible and Homosexual Practice, Gagnon

[28] Random House Unabridged Dictionary, © Random House, Inc. 2006.

[29] Genesis 19:8, New International Version © 1973, 1978, 1984 International Bible Society

[30] I Peter 4:3, Word Wealth

[31] Ezekiel 16:49, NIV

[32] Matthew 11:23-24 (general repentance); Mark 6:7-11 (lack of hospitality, rejection of Jesus' disciples)

[33] Josephus, *The Antiquities of the Jews* 1.200-201

[34] *Piylegesh* is the Hebrew word for concubine

[35] Compare this response of the Israelites to that of the men of Sodom. This lack of welcome was more expected in Sodom than amongst the Israelites!

[36] Sons of Belial (Biblical meaning is worthlessness) Belial is referred to as a demon in other ancient literature.

[37] Dr. Richard Mouw. © 2007 *For The Bible Tells Me So* docmentary.

[38] Ezekiel 16:49

[39] Leviticus 18:3

[40] Leviticus 20:10, Exodus 21:17, Exodus 31:14-

[41] Genesis 16:10

[42] Leviticus 18:19, 29-30

[43] Genesis 38:8, Exodus 21:10, Deut 25:5 and Psalms 78:63

[44] A kindred is a group of people related by blood or marriage.

[45] Harper's Bible Dictionary, edited by Paul J. Achtemier (San Francisco: Harper and Row, 1985)

[46] Genesis 29

[47] Matthew 19:6

[48] 2 Samuel 12:7-8

[49] Genesis 39:9

[50] Elwell, Walter A. "Entry for 'Concubine'". "Evangelical Dictionary of Theology". <http://www.biblestudytools.net/Dictionaries/BakerEvangelicalDictionary/bed.cgi?number=T154>. 1997.

[51] Concubinage. (2008, March 10). In Wikipedia, The Free Encyclopedia. Retrieved 01:03, April 10, 2008, from http://en.wikipedia.org/w/index.php?title=Concubinage&oldid=197331552

[52] Gesenius's Lexicon

[53] Genesis 35:22 & 49:4

[54] ©2003 David Guzik, Enduring Word Media.

[55] Matthew 19:6

[56] First Corinthians 7:2-5

[57] Augustine, "On the Goods of Marriage"

[58] Augustine, "Confessions"

[59] Acts 18:20

[60] New Spirit-Filled Life Bible, Romans, pg 1546; Executive Editor: Jack Hayford, Litt. D.; Associate Editors: Paul G. Chappell, Ph.D & Kenneth C. Ulmer, Ph. D., D.Min.

[61] Ibid.

[62] Ibid.

[63] Deuteronomy 6:4-5

[64] Exodus 20:3

[65] Romans 1:23, NKJV; (Gk. Anthrōpos)

[66] Idolatry. (2008, March 26). In *Wikipedia, The Free Encyclopedia*. Retrieved 18:58, March 26, 2008, from http://en.wikipedia.org/w/index.php?title=Idolatry&oldid=201063748

[67] Blue Letter Bible. "Dictionary and Word Search for akatharsia (Strong's 167)". Blue Letter Bible. 1996-2008. 12 Apr 2008. < http://cf.blueletterbible.org/lang/lexicon/lexicon.cfm?Strongs=G167&t=kjv >

[68] Exodus 32:19, Deuteronomy 9:16

[69] * (Note: The *Nestle-Aland and United Bible Societies* are "the most prominent modern Critical Text[s] of the Greek New Testament" according to the editors of the Spirit-Filled Life Bible. The *Nestle-Aland* is used as the basis of most contemporary New Testament translations, as well as being the standard for academic work in New Testament studies. The Greek text, as presented, is based on what biblical textual critics refer to as the "critical text". The critical text is an eclectic text compiled by a committee that examines a large number of manuscripts in order to

weigh which reading is thought closest to the *lost original*.) [Italics mine.]

[70] For further understanding of Jewish marital practices, see the *Old Testament Marriage* section in the chapter on Marriage and Adultery.

[71] Romans 1:24

[72] This word Aner was also used in Ephesisan 5:28 to describe how a **man** should treat his wife (or woman as it is also translated).

[73] First Corinthians 6:1-4

[74] First Corinthians 5:10-11

[75] First Corinthians 6:11

[76] Ephesians 5:23

[77] First Corinthians 6:18: "…he that committeth fornication sinneth against his own body." The Greek word for sinneth is hamartano which means to miss the mark.

[78] First Corinthians 6:19

[79] Dale G. Martin, Arsenokoites and Malakos: Meanings and Consequences ©2003 The Center for Lesbian and Gay Studies in Religion and Ministry (CLGS), retrieved 2008, April 4. from
http://www.clgs.org/5/5_4_3.html

[80] http://www.sacred-texts.com/cla/sib/index.htm

[81] Note: The original Sibylline Books were closely-guarded oracular scrolls written by prophetic priestesses (the Sibylls) in the Etruscan and early Roman Era as far back as the 6th Century B.C.E. These books were destroyed, partially in a fire in 83 B.C.E., and finally burned by order of the Roman General Flavius Stilicho (365-408 C.E.). There is very little knowledge of the actual contents of the original Sibylline Books. The texts which are presented here are forgeries, probably composed between the second to sixth century C.E. (taken from the http://www.sacred-texts.com/cla/sib/index.htm website)

[82] Sibylline Oracles 2.70-73, trans. J. J. Collins, in The Old Testament Pseudepigrapha, ed. James H.
Charlesworth [Garden City, NY: Doubleday, 1983]

[83] Dale G. Martin, Arsenokoites and Malakos:

[84] Eisegesis is the practice of interpreting scripture based on the interpreter's beliefs rather than the truthful meaning of the texts and/or words.

[85] Kirby, Peter. "Early Christian Writings" 2008, April 4 retrieved from
http://www.earlychristianwritings.com/text/actsjohn.html

[86] Ibid.

[87] Blue Letter Bible. "Dictionary and Word Search for malakos (Strong's 3120)". Blue Letter Bible. 1996-2008. 22 Mar 2008. < http://cf.blueletterbible.org/lang/lexicon/lexicon.cfm?Strongs=G3120&t=kjv >

[88] http://www2.evansville.edu/ecoleweb/glossary/clementr.html

[89] Prostitution in ancient Greece. (2008, March 19). In Wikipedia, The Free Encyclopedia. Retrieved 03:12,
  March 23, 2008, from http://en.wikipedia.org/w/
  index.php?title=Prostitution_in_ancient_Greece&oldid=199418456)

[90] Athenian pederasty. (2008, March 1). In Wikipedia, The Free Encyclopedia. Retrieved 03:07, March 23, 2008, from http://en.wikipedia.org/w/index.php?title=Athenian_pederasty&oldid=195109362

[91] One fragment of a Solon poem survives, in which he praises a 'boy in the lovely flower of youth, desiring his thighs and sweet mouth.' Young boys could be "deflowered" in the same manner as young virgin girls. 'Sweet mouth' refers to oral sex and 'desiring his thighs' refers to a sexual practice called intercural where a man does not anally penetrate a youth but instead rubs his penis between the youth's thighs from the rear for sexual pleasure. Both of these practices still exist today among adult men, the latter considered a form of 'safer sex'.

[92] Athenian Pederasty

[93] Kirby, Peter. "Early Christian Writings" 2008, April 4 retrieved from http://www.earlychristianwritings.com/text/actsjohn.html

[94] Kirby, Peter. "Early Christian Writings" 2008, April 4 retrieved from http://www.earlychristianwritings.com/text/actsjohn.html (Introduction)

[95] New International Version. (2008, March 15). In *Wikipedia, The Free Encyclopedia*. Retrieved 16:31,
  April 5, 2008, from http://en.wikipedia.org/w/index.php?title=
  New_International_Version&oldid=198354529

[96] First Corinthians 5:9; 5:10; 6:9

[97] New Spirit-Filled Life Bible, Copyright 2002 by Thomas Nelson, Inc., Pg 1578

[98] Jeremiah 3:14

[99] Mark 7:6-7

[100] John 4:24

[101] Down-low (slang). (2008, April 23). In *Wikipedia, The Free Encyclopedia*. Retrieved 17:48, April 25, 2008, from

http://en.wikipedia.org/w/index.php?title=Down-
low_%28slang%29&oldid=207514463

[102] John 4:27

[103] Bible, English, The Message © 2002 Eugene H. Patterson, Ephesians
4:11-15

[104] See Section on Romans 1

[105] The 11 verses of scripture comprise 0.035% of all scripture.

[106] Matthew 10:5-6, Matthew 15:22-24, John 7:35

[107] John 8:3-11

[108] Full story is in John 7:36-50. 'Go in Peace' can be translated 'go in
the way of peace or salvation'

[109] Matthew 22:39

[110] Blue Letter Bible. "Dictionary and Word Search for plēsion (Strong's
4139)". Blue Letter Bible. 1996-
2008. 8 Apr 2008. < http://
cf.blueletterbible.org/lang/lexicon/lexicon.cfm?Strongs=G4139&t=kjv >

[111] Matthew 22:40

[112] © 2007 *For The Bible Tells Me So* film

[113] John 13:25

[114] John 19:26, 20:2, 21:20

[115] Matthew 10:11

[116] Blue Letter Bible. "Dictionary and Word Search for *aspazomai (Strong's 782)*".
Blue Letter Bible. 1996-2008. 7 Nov 2008. < http://
www.blueletterbible.org/lang/lexicon/lexicon.cfm?
Strongs=G782&t=KJV >

[117] Luke 10:7

[118] Encyclopædia Britannica, Retrieved 2008, March 28 from
http://www.britannica.com/eb/article-9036351/gender-identity

[119] © 1993 Joseph Nicolosi, Healing Homosexuality

[120] Nicolosi, Reparative Therapy

[121] Nicolosi , Healing Homosexuality

[122] Nicolosi, Reparative Therapy

[123] Clay Aiken. (2008, October 23). In *Wikipedia, The Free
Encyclopedia*. Retrieved 05:08, October 23, 2008, from
http://en.wikipedia.org/w/index.php?title=Clay_Aiken&oldid=
247081259

[124] http://www.popcrunch.com/clay-aiken-gay-church-scandal-the-
central-christian-church-demands-assurance-clay-isnt-gay/

[125] Sheryl Swoopes and LZ Granderson, "Outside the Arc" article, ESPN Magazine, April 12, 2006. http://sports.espn.go.com/wnba/news/story?id=2204322

[126] © 2007 David Kinnaman and Fermi Project, unChristian: What a New Generation Really Thinks about Christianity… and Why It Matters

[127] Read Ephesians 2:5,8,9

[128] Mark 6:11

[129] Proverbs 3:5

[130] Deuteronomy 31:16; Hosea 1:2; Jeremiah 3:6-10

[131] Ephesians 4:29, NLT

[132] See the Section on Eunuchs in the Chapter "What did Jesus Say?"

[133] Civil Rights Act of 1964; Voting Rights Act of 1965

[134] Bayard Rustin. (2008, August 18). In *Wikipedia, The Free Encyclopedia*. Retrieved 17:24, August 29, 2008, from http://en.wikipedia.org/w/index.php?title=Bayard_Rustin&oldid=232696654

[135] AIDS Diagnoses data compiled from 33 states by CDC in 2006. http://www.cdc.gov/hiv/topics/surveillance/resources/slides/race-ethnicity/slides/race-ethnicity_12.pdf

[136] Left Behind – Black America: A neglected priority in the Global AIDS epidemic. Report by Black AIDS Institute. August 2008

[137] Ibid.

[138] T.D. Jakes. (2007, October 15) Black AIDS Institute website. Retrieved August 31, 2008, from http://www.blackaids.org/ShowArticle.aspx?articletype=SITEFEATURE&articleid=404&pagenumber=3

[139] LGBT Families to Meet with The Potter's House; http://www.soulforce.org/article/1363)

[140] Boykin, One More River to Cross, page 76

[141] http://www.ontheissues.org/Archive/2007_Dems_Howard_U_Health_Care.htm

[142] Noel Jones. December 24, 2007 *Promiscuous Sex Doesn't Cost Anything…But Your Life,* article written for Black AIDS Institute. http://www.blackaids.org/ShowArticle.aspx?pagename=ShowArticle&articletype=NEWS&articleid=455&pagenumber=1

Made in the USA
Lexington, KY
02 August 2014